£1·00

D0995637

# New Testament
# Commentary Survey

# New Testament Commentary Survey

*Fourth Edition*

## D. A. Carson

Inter-Varsity Press

 BakerBooks

A Division of Baker Book House Co
Grand Rapids, Michigan 49516

Copyright © 1993 by D. A. Carson

Published by
Inter-Varsity Press
38 De Montfort Street, Leicester, LE1 7GP, UK.

and

Baker Book House Company
P.O. Box 6287, Grand Rapids, MI 49516-6287

Printed in the United States of America

**British Library Cataloguing in Publication Data**

A catalogue record for this book is available from the British Library.

ISBN 0-85110-985-3

**Library of Congress Cataloging-in-Publication Data**

Carson, D. A.
    New Testament commentary survey / D.A. Carson. — 4th ed.
       p.    cm.
    ISBN 0-8010-2579-6
    1. Bible. N. T.—Commentaries—History and catechism. 2. Bible
N.T.—Commentaries—Bibliography. I. Title.
BS2341.C33    1993
016.2257—dc20                        93-12051

# Contents

# Preface

The first edition of this little book was written by Dr Anthony C. Thiselton, and appeared under the title *Personal Suggestions about a Minister's Library*. In 1973 it was revised, and shortly after that the "Best Buys" section was brought up to date. That revision also introduced a change in title and format: the *New Testament Commentary Survey* was born, the NT analogue of the *Old Testament Commentary Survey* (both published, at the time, exclusively by the British Theological Students Fellowship [TSF]). In 1976, I brought the book up to date again, simply by adding additional paragraphs and by inserting new prices and publishing information where relevant. Apart from such modifications, Dr Thiselton's comments were left unchanged. In 1984, TSF asked for another revision, and this time it was thought unwise simply to add a few more paragraphs. It seemed more sensible to recast the entire work, and enter it on a computer so that subsequent revisions, including price changes and the like, could be accomplished with relatively little work. With Dr Thiselton's kind permission, his text was sometimes incorporated into that third revision, occasionally with changes—especially on those rare occasions where I found myself mildly disagreeing with Dr Thiselton's assessment of a book. In America, Baker Book House brought out the third edition. There are now two analogous volumes on the OT—one prepared by John Goldingay for TSF in Britain, and one written by Tremper Longman III for Baker in the United States.

The fourth edition of this survey has been prepared a little earlier than originally envisaged, simply because the flood of commentaries that have appeared since the previous edition shows no sign of letting up. Moreover, prices and availability of commentaries have changed so dramatically during the past six or seven years that it seemed best to delay no longer.

The purpose of this short book is to provide theological students and ministers with a handy survey of the resources, especially commentaries, that are available in English to facilitate an understanding of the NT. The mature scholar is not in view. On the other hand, commentaries that are written at the popular level are generally given less attention than more substantive works. Theologically I am an evangelical, but many of the positive assessments offered in these notes are in connection with books written from the vantage point of some other theological tradition: the usefulness of a commentary often turns on something other than the theological stance of its author—assuming, of course, commentaries are read critically, as they should be, whatever one's theological heritage. Conversely, just because a commentary stands within the evangelical tradition does not necessarily mean that it is a good book. It may be thoroughly orthodox, but be poorly written, or uninformed, or quick to import from other biblical passages truths that cannot rightly be found in the texts on which comment is being offered. In other words, this survey is a guide to commentaries, not orthodoxy. Nevertheless I have not hesitated on occasion to draw attention to the theological "slant" of particular works. Such information is often as useful as comments on the work's level, general competence, and so forth. The restriction to English works is not absolute; occasionally I have included a foreign language work where nothing of a similar nature or stature exists in English. If I have not included more of them, it is because of my envisaged readership.

Most of the checking in preparation for this revision was done by my research assistant, Rev. Mark Krause, to whom I owe an enormous debt of gratitude—and not for his work on this project alone. Prices and other publication data are, I hope, both accurate and more or less comprehensive up to mid-1992.

Those interested in keeping up with the endless stream of commentaries need to consult the book review sections of journals. The *Expository Times* is often first off the mark, but its reviews are brief, and sometimes one is surprised by what books are left unmentioned. More comprehensive are the *Journal of Biblical Literature* and the *Catholic Biblical Quarterly*. Reviews that usually keep the theological student in mind, and which are written from an evangelical perspective, are found in *Themelios*. Other evangelical journals with useful reviews include *Churchman, Journal of the Evangelical Theological Society, Trinity Journal,* and *Westminster Theological Journal.* Students in search of tools for more advanced research should consult the excellent booklet edited by R. T. France, *A Bibliographical Guide to New Testament Research*, even though it is now badly dated. Older commentaries are treated to entertaining and sometimes profound comment in C. H. Spurgeon, *Commenting and Commentaries*, occasionally republished by BoT.

I have tried to scan the reviews of the third edition of this book, and learn from them. On some matters I remain unrepentant. If I do not devote more space to UBS productions, for instance, it is because many of their commentaries, although doubtless of value to Bible translators, are of minimal use to theological students and ministers. One reviewer thought some of my comments too trenchant. I have tried to be careful, but in a survey this brief I prefer to be a shade too trenchant than a good deal too bland. Two reviewers objected to the fact that I included my Matthew in the "Best Buys" section. Doubtless that was inexcusably poor judgment on my part. At the time, there were few full-scale commentaries on Matthew available within the evangelical tradition, so in the absence of competitors I thought the inclusion of my own work was justified. But I have changed my mind, and now on principle exclude anything I have written from "Best Buys." Apart from published reviews, I am indebted to several people who have written to me from various parts of the world to offer suggestions as to how to improve this survey. To all of them I extend my gratitude.

*Soli Deo gloria.*

D. A. Carson
Trinity Evangelical Divinity School
Summer 1992

# Abbreviations

Publishers named are those of the most recent editions in Britain and the United States. An entry such as (CUP) indicates that the book is published by CUP in both Britain and the United States. An entry with a "/"—for example, (IVP/Eerdmans)—indicates it is published by IVP in Britain and by Eerdmans in the United States. (SCM/) means it is published in Britain by SCM and not published in the United States; (/Doubleday) that it is published by Doubleday in the United States and not published in Britain. In the latter two cases, of course, local booksellers should not find it difficult to import the book from the foreign publisher (provided, of course, the work is still in print when you read these lines!). The same symbol, the "/", is also used on occasion to divide British and American dates, British and American prices, and so forth—always in that paired order.

Titles of commentaries are omitted when they are straightforward: for example, Leon Morris, *The Gospel according to John: The English Text with Introduction, Exposition and Notes*, will appear as *Leon Morris* (i.e., with the author's name in italic font, not the book title).

| | |
|---|---|
| AB | Anchor Bible (/Doubleday) |
| ACNT | Augsburg Commentary on the New Testament |
| ASV | American Standard Version |
| AV | Authorized Version |
| BECNT | Baker Exegetical Commentary on the New Testament |
| BIP | Books in Print |
| BNTC | Black's New Testament Commentaries [=HNTC] (Black/Harper, sometimes Hendrickson) |

| | |
|---|---|
| BoT | Banner of Truth |
| BST | The Bible Speaks Today (IVP/IVP) |
| CB | Century Bible |
| CBSC | Cambridge Bible for Schools and Colleges |
| CBC | Cambridge Bible Commentary on the NEB |
| CC | The Communicator's Commentary (/Word) |
| CGT | Cambridge Greek Testament (CUP) |
| CLC | Christian Literature Crusade |
| CNT | Commentaire du Nouveau Testament |
| CUP | Cambridge University Press |
| DSB | Daily Study Bible (St Andrew's Press/Westminster) |
| EB | The Expositor's Bible |
| EBC | The Expositor's Bible Commentary |
| EGGNT | Exegetical Guide to the Greek New Testament (/Eerdmans) |
| EGNT | Expositor's Greek New Testament |
| EKK | Evangelisch-katholisch Kommentar |
| ET | English Translation |
| EtBib | Etudes Bibliques |
| GNC | Good News Commentary (/Harper and Row) |
| hb | hardback |
| Hermeneia | Hermeneia: A Critical and Historical Commentary (SCM/Fortress) |
| HNTC | Harper's New Testament Commentaries [=BNTC] |
| HTKNT | Herders Theologisher Kommentar zum Neuen Testament (Herder) |
| IB | Interpreter's Bible (SPCK/Abingdon) |
| ICC | International Critical Commentary (T & T Clark/ sometimes Scribner's) |
| IFES | International Federation of Evangelical Students |
| IRT | Issues in Religion and Theology |
| KJV | King James Version |
| KPG | Knox Preaching Guides (/John Knox) |
| LBBC | Layman's Bible Book Commentaries (/Broadman) |
| LC | Layman's Bible Commentaries (SCM/John Knox) |
| MBS | Message of Biblical Spirituality (Glazier/ Liturgical) |
| MeyerK | Meyer Kommentar (Göttingen: Vandenhoeck und Ruprecht) |
| MMS | Marshall, Morgan and Scott |
| NCB | New Century Bible |
| nd | no date |
| NEB | New English Bible |

| | |
|---|---|
| NClar | New Clarendon Commentary on the NEB (OUP) |
| NIBC | New International Bible Commentary (/Hendrickson) |
| NIC (=NL) | New International Commentary (=New London) (some Hodder/all Eerdmans) |
| NIGTC | New International Greek Testament Commentary (Paternoster/Eerdmans) |
| NIV | New International Version |
| NL | New London Commentary: see NIC |
| np | no price known |
| NT | New Testament |
| NTC | New Testament Commentary (by Hendriksen and Kistemaker; BoT [for Hendriksen]/Baker; sometimes Evangelical Press [for Kistemaker]/Baker) |
| NTM | New Testament Message series (Veritas [Dublin]/ Glazier [Liturgical]) |
| NTSR | New Testament for Spiritual Reading |
| NTT | New Testament Theology (CUP) |
| o/p | out of print |
| OUP | Oxford University Press |
| pb | paperback |
| Pelican | Pelican Commentaries (Penguin, sometimes SCM/ Penguin, sometimes Westminster) |
| ProcC | Proclamation Commentaries (/Fortress) |
| REB | Revised English Bible |
| SBLMS | Society of Biblical Literature Monograph Series |
| SP | Scholars Press |
| SU | Scripture Union |
| s/h | second hand |
| SNTSMS | Society for New Testament Studies Monograph Series (CUP) |
| SacPag | Sacra Pagina |
| SP | Scholars Press |
| SUNY | State University of New York Press |
| SuppNovT | Supplements to Novum Testamentum |
| TBC | Torch Biblical Commentaries (SCM/Allenson) |
| TEV | Today's English Version |
| TNTC | Tyndale New Testament Commentaries (IVP/Eerdmans) |
| TOTC | Tyndale Old Testament Commentaries (IVP/Eerdmans) |
| TPI | Trinity Press International |
| TPINT | Trinity Press International New Testament Commentaries (SCM/TPI) |
| TSF | Theological Students' Fellowship |

| UBS | United Bible Societies |
|---|---|
| UPA | University Press of America |
| WBC | Word Biblical Commentary (/Word) |
| WC | Westminster Commentaries |
| WEC | The Wycliffe Exegetical Commentary (/Moody) |
| WUNT | Wissenschaftliche Untersuchungen zum Neuen Testament |

# 1

# Introductory Notes

## 1.1 The need for several types of commentary

For an effective teaching and preaching ministry, commentaries take their place among other essential tools. But since different kinds of tasks often require different types of tools, useful commentaries are of more than one kind. Those listed in this little book may serve in at least three or four distinct ways, which correspond to the following needs.

The dominant need is to understand meanings accurately. The issue at stake is that of sheer faithfulness to the biblical message, rather than smuggling one's own ideas into the interpretation under the cover of the authoritative text. Even so, commentaries in this category can be subdivided further. Some commentaries seek to establish the text and provide basic help in translation, choosing among variant readings and offering elementary help at the level of Greek syntax and semantics. Grammatical and linguistic commentaries help to ensure faithfulness to the meanings of words and phrases in their literary setting. Theological commentaries set words and phrases in the wider context of chapters, books, corpora, and even the canon. Of course, these three subcategories often overlap—indeed, they should do so, for it can be seriously misleading to try to understand a word or concept in isolation from its linguistic and theological context.

To understand a passage (let alone to expound it forcefully) very often requires a faithful and imaginative historical reconstruction of events. Actions and sayings cannot accurately be cashed into today's currency until the preacher (although not necessarily the congregation) has seen what these presuppose and involve in their original setting in the ancient world. The best response to those who argue that history, archaeology, and other related disciplines are irrelevant to the interpretative enterprise is to give them a copy of, say, Colin J. Hemer's *The Letters to the Seven Churches* (JSOT, 1986 / Eisenbrauns 1990), and suggest that they revise their theory. Moreover, rightly done this kind of study contributes toward a vivid, colorful, and honest reconstruction for the congregation or classroom. Admittedly it is disastrous when historical information becomes an end in intself (cf. the warning, "Divinity was easy; for 'divinity' meant Noah's Ark."). But even purely historical commentaries can do a useful job if they project readers faithfully into the ancient world.

Unfortunately, not a few commentaries in this camp attempt historical reconstructions that are long on speculation and short on even-handed weighing of evidence. Some of these historical reconstructions have become so powerful that they serve as a grid to authenticate the primary sources: for example, because a consensus has been reached among some scholars that early church history proceeded along certain lines, the biblical documents are forcefully squeezed into this theory and counterevidence is dismissed as anachronistic or the like. Moreover, these kinds of reconstructions are probably the most difficult theories for those not trained in the primary sources to evaluate.

Nevertheless, these commentaries often include histories of the text (including form- and redaction-critical analyses), plus information of a geographical, historical, cultic, and sociocultural nature that cannot easily be found and weighed elsewhere, without doing a lot of work in the primary sources.

Some commentaries offer useful guidance on the legitimate range of practical application. If one danger is to read one's own applications into the passage, books of the sort already mentioned may serve as the remedy. But equally, most students and pastors must be reminded of the many directions in which practical lessons may lie. Expository lecturing is not the same thing as expository preaching;

the Word must not only inform, but wound and heal, sing and sting. Some of the older commentaries are exemplary in their concern to apply the Scriptures to later readers; the DSB often offers invaluable suggestions. But these hints and helps must be reviewed in the light of strictly exegetical considerations, for practical concerns can so control the text that no one hears the Word of God. Worse, the search for relevance frequently degenerates into the trite or the trivial.

A few commentaries perform all of these functions, but they are rare, and usually dated.

## 1.2 Individual commentaries or series?

### 1.21 General principles

Series are almost always uneven, and the temptation to collect uniform sets of volumes should be seen for what it sometimes is. Often an author writes an individual volume because he or she has something to say that is worth saying. By contrast, series are often farmed out by publishers to well-known and therefore very busy scholars for whom the invitation is all part of a day's work. This does not call into question the value of any particular series; it is certainly not meant to brand all commentaries that belong to a series with the label of mediocrity. But it does mean that volumes in series should ideally be judged only on individual merit. Thus comments on the major NT series now available (e.g., BNTC/HNTC, ICC, Hermeneia, NIGTC, etc.) will be found not only in the following paragraphs, but below under individual authors. Sets prepared by one scholar are a different matter and are discussed below (1.4).

### 1.22 Series worth noting but not pursuing

A few series are worth identifying, even if only the exceptional volume in the series achieves mention in these pages. The *Living Word Commentary* (ed. E. Ferguson; Austin, Tex.: Sweet) testifies to the effort of the (noninstrumental) Churches of Christ to provide elementary commentaries for their laypersons. The series is in some ways theologically akin to TOTC/TNTC, but generally a shade lighter. It has no relation to the *Living Bible* except the similarity in name. It must also be distinguished from the *Living Word* series (IVP/), a series that is not so much an attempt at formal commentary as a series of lay-oriented expository studies full of application and life. *The Armoury*

*Commentary* is a compilation from various annual Bible Reading Notes of the Salvation Army over many years. *Everyman's Bible Commentary* (/Moody) is too elementary to be very useful; *The Layman's Bible Commentary* (/John Knox) is singularly undistinguished. Collins/ Fontana have come out with a series of thirteen books designed to explain "everything that really matters for the modern reader" of the NT. In some cases (e.g., Mark, Luke, John, Rom., Gal.), these are succinct commentaries on the TEV; elsewhere they provide essays (Acts) or brief introductions. They are elementary and sometimes misleading even if, on the whole, they are engagingly written. Fortress continues to publish its series *Proclamation Commentaries: The New Testament Witnesses for Preaching.* These short paperback books, written by established scholars, are supposed to help the preacher come to grips with the essential themes of the NT documents. Occasional volumes from the series are mentioned in these notes, but as a rule the commentaries are not very helpful to the preacher interested in systematically expounding the Scriptures, even if they are useful handbooks for helping students discover the way much contemporary scholarship understands the biblical texts. In short, they are useful compendia for students; preachers interested in biblical exposition should begin with something more challenging. The *Knox Preaching Guides* series is no better; the *Layman's Bible Book Commentary* (24 vols.; /Broadman) is very elementary, and frequently resorts to slippery language to sound more conservative than it really is. The *Communicator's Commentary Series* (/Word) is a trifle better than those just mentioned, partly because the individual volumes are usually longer than those in the other series; but application is read back into the text with alarming frequency and with too little awareness of the hermeneutical steps being taken. At best these commentaries are worth a quick skim after the preacher's serious exegetical work is well in hand, in order to retrieve any homiletical stimulus that may be present. Other series too thin to merit much notice in these pages include the *Collegeville Bible Commentary Series*. A new set, The *Complete Biblical Library*, edited by Ralph W. Harris (Springfield, Mo.: Gospel, 1991), is an extraordinary mélange. It includes an expanded interlinear (the textus receptus plus "important variants"), its own text-critical apparatus, various versions, and verse-by-verse commentary designed for the beginning layperson. In other words, the more technical material is almost useless to the lay reader, and the comments are so lacking in depth as to be almost useless to any mature reader, lay or otherwise. Some sections are better than others, but the series as a whole is too expensive ($639.20) for the little it offers. *The Free Will Baptist Commentary* (/Randall House) includes one or two volumes worth a quick skim (e.g., Jack W. Stallings on John), but is so elementary and so defensive on "free will" that it can safely be overlooked.

## 1.23 More substantial series

Better known and more substantial series, whose individual volumes normally receive separate treatment in the pages of this book, include the following:

The *Anchor Bible* (/Doubleday) is a decidedly mixed series. It is ecumenical, moderately critical, and designed to extend through both Testaments and the Apocrypha. Each volume offers introduction, a new translation, linguistic and exegetical notes, and sometimes a more detailed exposition. But the length and complexity of the treatment vary enormously: for example, Brown on John and on the Johannine Epistles is immensely detailed, while Albright and Mann on Matt. have produced a volume with a lengthy introduction and almost no exegesis.

The series of *Black New Testament Commentaries / Harper New Testament Commentaries* aims to provide lucid comment on the NT text and a fresh translation, without requiring a detailed knowledge of Greek. A few of the volumes in the series are distinguished (e.g., Barrett on 1–2 Corinthians). On the American side some of the volumes in the series are apparently being taken over by Hendrickson.

The *Broadman Bible Commentary* is a product of scholars related to the Southern Baptist Convention (SBC). The series is compact, expository, not technical, not particularly insightful, frequently bland, sometimes speculative. The reformation now taking place in the ranks of the SBC has dictated that an alternative and more conservative series, *The New American Commentary*, be produced by the same press. Only a few volumes have so far appeared. Its authors have been drawn from Baptist ranks both within and outside the SBC. The early volumes are generally competent enough, pitched at a middle level.

The *Epworth Preachers Commentaries* are a series of commentaries more exegetical than expository, but too brief to be of great help. It appears that the series may be taking on new life: after several years with no new volume, Kenneth Grayston's work on John has recently appeared. It is more interested in narrative structures than in helping preachers, but is certainly worth scanning.

The *Expositor's Bible Commentary* (/Zondervan) is a twelve-volume work of large pages and small print designed to offer exegetical and expository comment on the entire Bible, using the NIV text as the basis. The NT portion embraces volumes 8–12. The series is committed to evangelicalism, but suffers serious unevenness—a flaw made worse by the fact that more than one NT book commentary is bound in each volume (e.g., the Synoptics in vol. 8, John and Acts in vol. 9, etc.). It is usually more technical than the old EB (1887–96).

Although seriously dated, the five volumes of the old *Expositor's Greek New Testament* are still worth owning and reading, along with more recent works. Pick it up s/h, or from the publisher (/Eerdmans 1952; $89.95 the set).

*Hermeneia* (SCM/Fortress) is a full-scale critical commentary series that devotes considerable attention to parallel texts. Unlike the ICC, allowance is made for readers without a classical education, by providing translations (usually from the Loeb edition) of cited Greek and Latin authors. Several of the volumes are translations of German works, and this includes some extremely dated books (e.g., Bultmann on the Johannine Epistles, Haenchen on John). "Parallelomania" (to use Sandmel's famous expression) and a naive appeal to history-of-religions assumptions frequently surface, but the series is invaluable for the serious exegete and expositor. A few volumes are outstanding (e.g., Attridge on Hebrews).

The *International Critical Commentary*, a turn-of-the-century project that is now being renewed, includes some major commentaries that still set a high standard, even if they are now rather dated. Greek and Latin texts are cited without translation; this will prove a drawback to many modern readers. Only a few volumes of the modern updating have appeared, but they are of exceptional quality (see notes on Cranfield on Romans, Davies and Allison on Matthew)—although so expensive as to be beyond the reach of many students and pastors.

The *Interpretation* series of commentaries (/John Knox) focuses less on detailed exegesis than on the thrust and themes of the biblical books, presented in a way best calculated to help the preacher and to relate the text to a wider context. The aim is admirable; the execution is mixed, partly because the thinness of the exegesis sometimes allows room for rather too much speculation.

The *Interpreter's Bible* (SPCK/Abingdon) is a well intended but largely failed project to mingle historical scholarship and homiletical hints.

The IVP *New Testament Commentaries* (/IVP) are designed to fit into the fairly narrow slot between TNTC and BST—in other words, they are still commentaries, but they are brief and simple, and designed to be immediately nurturing. Of the three that have appeared so far, only one deserves special praise (I. Howard Marshall on 1 Peter).

The *Moffatt* series, with rare exceptions, is not much more than a major disappointment.

The *New Century Bible* (MMS/Eerdmans) normally adopts a moderately critical stance. Primary attention is devoted to understanding what the text says, without raising many broader theological, expository, or other concerns. Some of the volumes in the series are dry; a few offer excellent value for the money.

The *New International Biblical Commentary* (/Hendrickson) has adapted the old GNC series to the NIV, and is gradually adding new volumes. On the whole it is competent without being technical or overly long.

The *New Testament Message* series (/Michael Glazier) is a Catholic series of slim books that vary between being more-or-less commentaries (working through the text roughly paragraph by paragraph) and more-or-less thematic surveys.

A new series of *Narrative Commentaries* (Epworth/TPI) may become, in the NT, the American equivalent of the revised *Epworth Preachers Commentaries*. Only one volume has so far appeared in both forms, that of Kenneth Grayston on John.

The *New Clarendon Bible* on the NEB has ground to a halt. Only a few volumes were published, and no more are projected. That is probably a good thing: the books that appeared were too brief and too bland to be useful—again with one or two notable exceptions.

The *New International Commentary on the New Testament* (/Eerdmans; sometimes referred to in the UK as the *New London Commentary*, MMS/) is a still incomplete series of commentaries that adopts conservative critical views and is concerned to offer an exegesis of the Scriptures themselves. The text of these commentaries demands no special knowledge; the footnotes presuppose some knowledge of Greek and (occasionally) Hebrew and Latin. With the death of F. F. Bruce, its editor for many years, editorial direction has passed to Gordon D. Fee, who is commissioning writers not only to complete the series but to prepare new volumes to replace some of the older entries. In this new form, Fee has set a high standard with his own work on 1 Corinthians.

The *New International Greek Testament Commentary* (Paternoster/Eerdmans) is up-to-date, bibliographically almost exhaustive, exegetical, and broadly within the evangelical tradition. Only a few volumes have appeared so far; several more are slated for publication shortly. One or two volumes have been criticized, not unfairly, by clergy who find their contents too technical and tightly packed to be useful. For clergy and others well trained in Greek and exegesis, the series is one to watch.

The *Pelican* series is generally undistinguished, but it boasts a few commentaries that are quite outstanding, including Sweet's work on the Apocalypse (now available in the USA under the TPI *New Testament Commentary* series).

The *Pillar Commentary Series* (/Eerdmans) started life as a non-series. Eerdmans published three independent commentaries (Carson on John, Morris on Romans, Hughes on Revelation) and put them all in the same binding. They then decided it was worth filling out an entire series, and the other NT books have now been commissioned.

*Sacra Pagina* is a new series edited by Daniel J. Harrington, S.J. (/Michael Glazier). The two or three volumes released so far reflect the best of modern critical Catholic scholarship. The commentaries include fresh translation, critical analysis, and theologically sensitive exposition within the Roman Catholic tradition.

The *Standard Bible Studies* series (/Standard Publishing) is a series of commentaries designed for the ordinary reader. Most of them reflect a very poor level of competence. The volume by Paul R. McReynolds on Mark is an attractive exception.

The *Torch Bible Commentaries* are brief, exegetical, sometimes theological; but frequently the help they provide is too lean precisely where it is most needed.

The *Tyndale New Testament Commentaries* are designed for the mythical well-read layperson, but many pastors profit as well. The series is conservative, but focuses most attention on explaining the meaning of the text, with minimal interaction with the voluminous secondary literature. Originally based on the AV/KJV, with Greek and Hebrew transliterated and explained, the series is being rewritten based on the RSV or NIV (at the individual author's discretion), and space is being assigned more equitably. Several of the volumes of this new edition are, within the constraints of the series, outstanding (e.g., Marshall on Acts).

The *Wesleyan Bible Commentary* is a six-volume work published in 1979, and reprinted in 1986 (/Hendrickson). It is "a set of commentaries within the Wesleyan frame of reference," and uses the ASV. The series is not technical, and most sections are written with warmth and piety. Unfortunately, the competence of the authors is quite variable, and most of the work was seriously dated before it went to press.

The *Westminster Commentaries* are dull, dated, and dry.

The *Word Biblical Commentary* is a full-scale series that aims to cover every book in the Bible. Many of the NT volumes have appeared. The series offers fresh translation, an original (and sometimes annoyingly repetitive) format, thoughtful interaction with the literature, and a commitment to handle both exegetical and literary/critical concerns. A few of the volumes that have appeared are already standard reference works. Do not let the "evangelical" label fool you: although some of the contributors sit comfortably within that tradition, in other cases the label applies only by the most generous extension.

## 1.24 One-volume multiauthor commentaries

One-volume commentaries are too brief to be useful in detailed exegesis and exposition, but they have the considerable advantage of providing at least something on every book of the Bible—a special advantage when the student or minister is young or able to maintain only a very small library. *The New Bible Commentary* (IVP/Eerdmans, rev. ed. 1970) is condensed, evangelical, and brief. It is primarily exegetical, but a little space is devoted to discussing critical theories and occasionally to ongoing application of the text. It has become something of a standard around the English-speaking world among evangelical readers of single-volume commentaries, but is now seriously dated. A new, completely rewritten edition, based on the NIV, is scheduled to appear very shortly. Several other volumes have aimed for more or less the same market. Perhaps the only one that should be mentioned here is *A Bible Commentary for Today* (Pickering and Inglis/ 1979) or *The New Layman's Bible Commentary* (/Zondervan 1979), a product of the Christian Brethren. Based on the RSV, its focus is sometimes on exegesis, sometimes on exposition. On the whole it is lighter than NBC. One should not overlook the latest revision, edited by F. F. Bruce—the *International Bible Commentary* (/Zondervan 1986).

Until fairly recently, the standard one-volume mainstream critical commentary was probably *Peake's Commentary* (Nelson, rev. ed. 1962; now published by Routledge 1991 £40.00/). It should not be confused with the 1919 edition, still sold s/h. Nowadays, however, it has been eclipsed by *Harper's Bible Commentary* (Harper and Row, 1990/1988); *The Interpreter's One-Volume Commentary on the Bible* (/Abingdon), not to be confused with IB; and especially *The New Jerome Biblical Commentary* (G. Chapman/Prentice Hall 1989/1990). The latter two also treat the Apocrypha.

In a class by itself is the *Women's Bible Commentary*, ed. by Carol A. Newson and Sharon H. Ringe (/Westminster & John Knox, 1992). It is not a commentary on the whole Bible, but on those passages and themes that either mention women or are judged by the authors to be of special relevance to women. Thus the section on John treats 2:1–11; 4:4–42; 7:53–8:11; 11:1–44; 12:1–9; 19:25–27; 20:1–18 (so far as Mary Magdalene is the focus of interest), and offers comments on, for example, the use of "Father" for addressing God. Despite some excellent insights here and there, the work as a whole is far less interested in hearing what Scripture says than in using it to bless the controlling axioms of the more radical edge of the feminist movement.

## 1.3 Older commentaries

The present notes tend to concentrate on recent books, especially since useful guides are available to the older classics (e.g., the guide by Spurgeon). On the Greek text, some of the older commentators, including Westcott and Lightfoot, tended to overlook the distinctive fluidity of Hellenistic Greek as over against the more precisely defined constructions of the classical era; that aside, to those whose Greek is reasonably good they always repay careful study. G. Wilson has compiled "digests of Reformed comment" on most of the NT books. Published in pb by BoT (whose prices, especially in the UK, remain gratifyingly low), these slim volumes provide useful distillations of Calvin and other majesterial Reformers, and of some of the Puritans, with occasional snippets from more recent writers (including Lightfoot and Stott). The comments are often apposite and spiritually stimulating, but of course these books must be used in conjunction with major exegetical works. Zondervan recently reprinted J. P. Lange's commentaries in twelve volumes, but it is again o/p.

Klock and Klock, which used to serve us well with limited edition reprints of important commentaries, is now listed in BIP as "Inactive/Out-of-Business." Apparently some stock has been taken over by Kregel. Some of the commentaries mentioned in the last edition of this survey are now regrettably o/p, including P. Fairbairn on the Pastorals, F. J. A. Hort on 1 Peter, and James B. Mayor on James.

Some patristic commentaries are bound up with volumes of *The Ante-Nicene, Nicene and post-Nicene Fathers.* Calvin's commentaries are available in various reprint editions of older translations. Perhaps the least expensive access is in the twelve-volume edition of Eerdmans ($21.95 per vol.; $260.00 the set). Some of Calvin's commentaries are available from BoT. Matthew Henry's work, originally written to complement the work of Matthew Poole, is available, on the British side, in a one-volume edition from Marshall Pickering (£24.95), and in a two-volume pb from Hodder (£3.95 each). On the American side, both Zondervan and Hendrickson have produced one-volume editions ($29.95 and $34.95, respectively). Marshall Pickering / Zondervan are about to introduce a modernized edition of Matthew Henry that many readers will doubtless appreciate. Both Calvin and Henry are still worth reading. The latter makes shrewd, practical comments; the former is a more reliable interpreter of Scripture. Both should be used only in conjunction with modern commentators.

## 1.4 One-author sets

A. T. Robertson's *Word Pictures of the New Testament* (6 vols.; /Baker $89.95) provides comments on the more important Greek words of the NT text, in a way that often brings them to life, but sometimes he is dangerously near irresponsible etymologizing (cf. the warnings of James Barr in his *The Semantics of Biblical Language*). Only rarely, however, is there a howler. The magnificent achievement of H. A. W. Meyer in the last century has been reprinted in ET: eleven fat volumes with a total of 7050 pp. (/Hendrickson $250). Of course these commentaries should not be used independently of more recent ones.

J. C. Ryle's *Expository Thoughts on the Gospels* are still being reprinted—in seven volumes by BoT (/$59.95, or $8.95 per vol.), in four volumes (Evangelical Press/Baker £22.95 pb/$95.00), and in three volumes (J. Clarke/, Matthew–Mark in the same volume; £35.00/). The series is devout, militantly Protestant, and down-to-earth. His thoughts are simple (often too simple) but telling. At least they are thoroughly practical, and directly serve the preacher.

Albert Barnes' *Notes on the New Testament* (/Kregel in one vol., $44.95; /Baker in 14 vols., $298.00) marries common sense and pungent practicality, but every so often resorts to eccentric exegesis. C. Erdman's seventeen volumes on the NT (o/p) are lightweight, but sometimes worth a quick skim. R. C. H. Lenski's twelve-volume *The Interpretation of the New Testament* (/Augsburg-Fortress $295.00, $27.95 per vol.) aims to force the student to think through the Greek text and stimulate exegetical rigor, but his grasp of Greek is mechanical, without respect for the fluidity of Greek in the Hellenistic period. The series is marred by a militant or even angry tone in defense of orthodox Lutheranism.

William Barclay's *Daily Study Bible* covers the entire NT in eighteen volumes. The second revised edition is available on both sides of the Atlantic (St. Andrews/Westminster & John Knox £78.00 pb or £4.50 per vol. / $245.00 hb or $14.95 per vol.; $145.95 pb or $8.95 per vol.). Its value for the expositor is enormous; Barclay is eminently quotable and could not be dull if he tried. But two tendencies should be noted by way of warning: Barclay often maximizes "spiritual" application from the text after minimizing the historical foundation (e.g., miracles tend to be lessons rather than events); and sometimes one wonders whether the text bears all the applications suggested. But the minister who can find foundations elsewhere will enjoy Barclay's superstructure, even if some of the more dashing frescoes should be ignored.

A series not worth purchasing is the eighteen-volume *Renaissance New Testament* by Randolph O. Yeager (/Pelican $25.00 per vol.). Each hb volume is close to 600 pp. long, and the series occupied Yeager for fifty years; but the result is a disappointing monument to misplaced energy. The work is based on the KJV; many Greek words have concordance references provided for them, duplicating tools that already exist; most terms are parsed. The comments are shallow, the prose turgid, comment on Greek syntax too frequently misguided.

Considerably better is the series of commentaries by William Hendriksen (NTC). Eight volumes are in print: Matthew, Mark, Luke, John, Romans, Galatians–Ephesians, Philippians–Colossians–Philemon, Thessalonians–Timothy–Titus (BoT, ranging in price from £12.95 to £19.95 [BoT does not list the Romans vol.] / Baker, ranging from $22.95 to $29.95). Hendriksen is self-consciously orthodox and Reformed. Although his comments are often helpful to the expositor, the verbosity of his style and the selectivity of his interaction with alternative interpretations demand that he be supplemented with other works. Nevertheless his concern for practical application can make his work useful to some preachers. In the wake of Hendriksen's death, Simon Kistemaker has agreed to complete the series, four volumes of which have now appeared: Acts, Hebrews, James–Johannine Epistles, 1–2 Peter and Jude (/Baker, ranging from $18.95 to $29.95). On the British side, only the volume on Hebrews has been picked up (Evangelical Press/ £12.95). On the whole his work is solid but not incisive, with the result that there are usually better alternatives. His volume on Acts is probably his best.

# 2

# Supplements
# to the Commentaries

In the first two editions of this little book, a few notes were included in this chapter offering bibliographical suggestions on parables, NT theologies, Bible and theological dictionaries, and one or two other matters. In the third edition, I eliminated such notes, since the work focuses primarily on commentaries, and to include many other matters would demand that this section be greatly expanded to be responsible, with some criteria given regarding the topics covered. I have retained only two subsections: one dealing with NT introductions and another with NT theologies.

## 2.1 New Testament introductions

Pride of place must go to the mammoth work by Donald Guthrie, *New Testament Introduction*, now in its fourth edition (1990; IVP £24.95 / IVP $39.95). There are few critical questions Guthrie does not discuss. His style is invariably irenic, his conclusions normally traditional. Relatively little space is given to the theological contribution of each NT book, or to struggling with the actual history of early

Christianity. Occasionally the sheer volume of detail may make it difficult for students to sort out what is most important. A somewhat more compact work, designed to serve as a textbook (500 pp.) for theological students, is *An Introduction to the New Testament* by D. A. Carson, Douglas J. Moo, and Leon Morris (1992 IVP np / Zondervan $24.95). It is not as comprehensive as Guthrie, but for some students that may be an advantage.

The mainstream critical work is still that of Werner Georg Kümmel: *Introduction to the New Testament* (Abingdon $21.95 / SCM £15.00). The comprehensiveness of the topics discussed, in relatively little space, means that far too many opinions are advanced without defense. But no introduction is quite like it for disciplined compression, and it will be consulted again and again. The standard Roman Catholic *New Testament Introduction* is by Alfred Wikenhauser (o/p). An alternative evangelical *Introduction to the New Testament* is that of Everett F. Harrison (/Eerdmans 1964 $29.95). The work is far simpler and shorter than those of Guthrie and Carson/Moo/Morris, but it is now seriously dated. The two volumes by Ralph P. Martin, *New Testament Foundations: A Guide for Christian Students* (Paternoster 1985–86, £10.25 and £11.75 respectively / Eerdmans o/p), attempt to mingle traditional questions of introduction, including historical and cultural background, with an emphasis on the theological message of the NT books. The advantage is that it brings together material not normally bound up in one (or two) volumes; the disadvantage is that in some ways the work falls between two stools. Not a few of its judgments belong to the central stream of critical thought.

At opposite ends of the critical spectrum stand two works on critical introduction. Neither owes anything to distinctively "evangelical" tradition, and together they demonstrate how confusing such categories as "liberal" and "conservative" can be. The second edition of *The New Testament: An Introduction* by Norman Perrin and Dennis C. Duling (Harcourt Brace Jovanovich 1982 £13.95 pb/$15.00 pb) fits the NT documents into a doctrinaire history of NT Christianity reconstructed at the beginning of the book. The result is a pretty radical scheme. At the other end stands John A. T. Robinson's *Redating the New Testament* (/TPI nd $19.95), which argues that all the books in the NT canon were complete before A.D. 70, and that external ascriptions of authorship in early Christian tradition are remarkably accurate. Both books deserve careful reading by the serious student, if only to discover how data can be made to fit such wildly different schemes.

Six introductions are cast in somewhat independent molds, as judged by what they add to the discussion of traditional introduction. One of the most helpful to the student is the short book by Bruce M. Metzger, *The New Testament: Background, Growth and Content* (/Abingdon 1965 $19.95). Somewhat more detailed, and focusing on the factors that produced the NT documents, is C. F. D. Moule's *The Birth of the New Testament* (3d ed.; Black 1981 £12.99/Harper o/p). Much more ambitious is the two-volume work by Helmut Koester, *Introduction to the New Testament*: vol. 1: *History, Culture, and Religion of the Hellenistic Age*; vol. 2: *History and Literature of Early Christianity* (De Gruyter 1982 $34.95). The first volume condenses a massive amount of useful material, with only occasional places where another viewpoint might have been desirable (e.g., a too confident assumption of the pre-Christian roots of full-fledged Gnosticism, and a comparatively thin treatment of the Jewish sources). The second volume is extraordinarily tendentious, standing self-consciously in the history-of-religions school as understood by Rudolph Bultmann, to whom the work is dedicated. It is not just that radical positions are taken (e.g., very little is said about Jesus because like his mentor Koester feels that there is little the historian can say about him) but that bibliographies are one-sided, and extreme positions are put forward as if no other approach to the evidence were possible. For that reason the second volume should not be used by a student just breaking into the problems of NT introduction. A somewhat similar approach is adopted by Christopher Rowland's *Christian Origins: An Account of the Setting and Character of the Most Important Messianic Sect of Judaism* [the American subtitle was *From Messianic Movement to Christian Religion*] (SPCK 1985 £16.00 / Augsburg o/p), with results only slightly less radical. Unlike Koester, who sees Christianity's roots in the Greco-Roman world, Rowland sees those roots in apocalyptic. *The Introduction to the New Testament* by Charles B. Puskas (/Hendrickson 1989 $19.95) barely addresses traditional questions of introduction, but deals with backgrounds of the NT (Greco-Roman, Jewish, language, text), methods for interpreting the NT (various historical methods, genre criticism), and the formation of early Christianity. Although there is a fair bit of useful material here, Puskas frequently adopts standard critical conclusions as if they were uncontested "givens," so that his work is less valuable than it might have been. Finally, one should mention Raymond F. Collins' *Introduction to the New Testament* (SCM 1983 £9.50 pb / Doubleday 1987 $10.95 pb), which is less concerned with traditional matters of introduction than with the formation and closing of the canon, the use of major literary tools used in NT study, and an attempt to reconcile his approach with his own Roman Catholic tradition. Perhaps what these books unambiguously show is that an "introduction" to the NT now means different things to different people.

To notes on these six works should be added a mention of the spate of books concerned to relate the findings of cultural anthropology and sociology to matters of NT introduction and exegesis. In particular, one thinks of Bruce J. Malina's *The New Testament World: Insights from Cultural Anthropology* (SCM 1983 £5.95 pb / Westminster-John Knox 1985 $19.95 pb); Wayne A. Meeks's *The First Urban Christians* (Yale 1983 hb £40.00 / o/p; 1984 pb £12.00/$14.00); Derek J. Tidball's *An Introduction to the Sociology of the New Testament* (o/p). In two of the three cases, some of the best ideas have been borrowed from the writings of Prof. E. A. Judge, usually published as essays in obscure places.

Finally, there is a plethora of purely popular introductions that will receive no mention here, and of older works that are worth consulting from time to time. The latter include: James Moffatt's *An Introduction to the Literature of the New Testament* (o/p); A. H. McNeile's *An Introduction to the Study of the New Testament* (o/p); J. Gresham Machen's *The New Testament: An Introduction to its Literature and History* (BoT repr.1976 £6.50), pitched at a fairly elementary level; and Theodor Zahn's majesterial three-volume *Introduction to the New Testament* (/Kregel nd $49.95).

## 2.2 New Testament theologies

In this section I am excluding the myriad of studies that examine only one part of the NT canon, such as studies on the theology of Paul, say, or of John. I am including only those major recent attempts at biblical theology that tackle the entire NT. For a survey of the history and central problems in NT theology, one cannot do better than to read Gerhard F. Hasel's *New Testament Theology: Basic Issues in the Current Debate* (/Eerdmans $8.95 pb). For a history of the rise of current critical positions that touch both NT introduction and NT theology, see Stephen Neill's *The Interpretation of the New Testament*

*1861–1986*, second edition brought up to date (1961–1986) by N. T. Wright (OUP 1988 pb £7.95/$13.95), and Werner G. Kümmel's *The New Testament: The History of the Investigation of its Problems* (o/p). A profound though regrettably skeptical discussion of the nature of NT theology is provided by Robert Morgan's *The Nature of New Testament Theology* (o/p).

Three substantial NT theologies have been penned in recent years by scholars within the evangelical tradition. The first, by George Eldon Ladd, *A Theology of the New Testament* (Lutterworth 1975 £13.95 / Eerdmans 1974 $24.95), is a comprehensive study that is better in Paul and John than in the Synoptics. Even in the latter, Ladd's treatment of eschatology and salvation history is competent. It is in the failure to distinguish different emphases among the Synoptic Gospels that one could long for more in Ladd's work. The second volume, *New Testament Theology* by Donald Guthrie (IVP 1981 £21.95 / IVP 1981 $39.95) is a mammoth volume. Unlike Ladd, who attempts to synthesize the theology of each of the corpora in turn, Guthrie handles theme after theme found in the NT, and goes through each corpus for each theme. Perhaps there is not as much synthesis for each theme as one might expect: the price paid for this otherwise attractive format is that the reader finishes his or her study without much of an idea of, say, Paul's distinctive contribution to NT theology as a whole, but only of his contribution to certain themes. The third effort, Leon Morris's *New Testament Theology* (/Zondervan 1986 $20.95), is much briefer and more elementary, virtues that may commend themselves to those approaching NT theology for the first time.

The record of major disappointments from the past includes George Barker Stevens' *The Theology of the New Testament* (T & T Clark 1918 /$29.95) and Charles Caldwell Ryrie's *Biblical Theology of the New Testament* (/Moody o/p).

More broadly, Rudolf Bultmann's *Theology of the New Testament* (Macmillan 1951 $24.00 pb / SCM in 2 vols.: vol. 1=1971, £12.50; vol. 2=1965, £9.50) still repays close reading. The work has proved seminal and provocative, and for this reason it is constantly praised. Yet as stimulating as it is, the work is overrated. The very fertility of Bultmann's ideas is far too often founded on naked antitheses that fly in the face of the evidence, and the beginning student must constantly remember that precisely when Bultmann is at his most quotable he seldom means what the student thinks he does, because the theological terms have become for Bultmann a set of codes which, stripped of the myths that allegedly adhere to them, convey a shockingly naturalistic existentialism. Hans Conzelmann's *An Outline of the Theology of the New Testament* (o/p) adheres to the same tradition, but because it was designed to serve as a classroom text it is a little more approachable.

A frequently overlooked but very valuable work is that of Ethelbert Stauffer, *New Testament Theology* (o/p). The book is relatively brief, very condensed, wisely cautious about the significance of Greco-Roman parallels while reflecting considerable learning in the area. Scarcely less valuable is W. G. Kümmel's *The Theology of the New Testament* (SCM 1976 £12.50 / o/p). Kümmel focuses on the "major witnesses" (Jesus, Paul, and John), with briefer consideration of other sources. Kümmel finds unity and a strong Lutheran tradition in consistent NT testimony to God's eschatological salvation in Jesus Christ. Better yet is the two-volume work by Leonhard Goppelt, *Theology of the New Testament*, vol. 1: *The Ministry of Jesus in its Theological Significance*, and vol. 2: *The Variety and Unity of the Apostolic Witness to Christ* (/Eerdmans, 1981 and 1983, $16.95 and $18.95 respectively). Goppelt's work is perhaps still the best exposition of a "salvation history" frame of reference to NT interpretation. More difficult to assess, because incomplete, is the *New Testament Theology* of Joachim Jeremias, who managed only one volume, *The Proclamation of Jesus* (SCM 1973 £12.00 / Macmillan 1977 $40.00), before his death. Jeremias is at his best in teasing out the significance of the various language forms of Jesus; his work on parables, much praised in former years, has now been superseded.

# 3

# Individual Commentaries

## 3.01 Matthew

After some years of relatively thin pickings, the Gospel of Matthew now enjoys the support of several substantial commentaries, all published during the last decade. Pride of place should go to the new ICC commentary by *W. D. Davies* and *Dale C. Allison*. The first volume appeared in 1988 (T & T Clark £29.95/$59.95), covering introduction and chapters 1–7. The second volume, on chapters 8–18, was published in 1991 (T & T Clark £29.95/$49.95). The third and final volume has yet to appear. This work is moderately critical, and leaves few stones unturned. Its attention to detail sometimes leaves the flow of Matthew's argument less than clear, and its exorbitant price will put it out of the range of many buyers. *Daniel J. Harrington*'s Sac-Pag work (/Michael Glazier 1992 $19.95) is the most recent major (and completed!) commentary on Matt. It adopts mainstream positions. It is well written, but thinner on theology than one might have expected for a book of this size. *D. A. Carson* in the EBC series (vol.8, bound with Mark and Luke; /Zondervan 1984 $34.95) is larger than the normal parameters allowed for that series, and, within the evangelical tradition, attempts to explain the text while interacting with the most significant of the recent literature. A shorter but useful commentary within the evangelical tradition is that of *Robert H. Mounce* (NIBC; 1991 $9.95). Pitched at about the same level, roughly mainstream in its theological orientation, but fully condensed and insightful in terms of exegesis, is *Robert H. Smith* (ACNT; 1989 $16.95 pb). The TNTC commentary by *R. T. France* (1986/1987 £4.95/$9.95) is outstanding, although not many will follow him in his interpretation of the eschatological discourse.

Other substantial commentaries from the past decade, each slightly off the beaten track, include the following five. *Robert H. Gundry* (/Eerdmans o/p) is the most rigorously redaction-critical commentary on Matthew yet to appear. It detects a "midrashic" approach to the Jesus tradition at many points (although without ever telling us whence the definition and formal characteristics of midrash are derived). Gundry has chosen to interact with few secondary sources. Few preachers will find it serviceable in sermon preparation. The commentary by *Francis W. Beare* (/Harper 1982 $29.95) is more traditional in its layout, but rather skeptical in many of its historical judgments. Worse, its bibliography and discussion were at least fifteen years out of date the day the work was published. *Daniel Patte* (Augsburg-Fortress 1987/1986 £20.25 pb/$21.95 pb) shows his interest in his subtitle: *A Structural Commentary on Matthew's Faith.* Frederick Dale Bruner has produced two volumes in which, again, the subtitle helps to explain the author's purpose: *The Christbook: A Historical/Theological Commentary,* vol. 1: Matthew 1–12; vol. 2: Matthew 13–28 (/Word, 1987 & 1990, $24.95 & np respectively). Despite a substantial amount of useful theological discussion, the work can be challenged rather frequently at the exegetical level. Finally, Samuel Tobias Lachs has written *A Rabbinic Commentary on the New Testament: The Gospels of Matthew, Mark, and Luke* (/Ktav 1987 $39.50 hb & $19.95 pb).

Before turning to more commentaries, I should mention three books which, while not commentaries, have special value for the study of Matthew The first, a brief volume edited by Graham Stanton, *The Interpretation of Matthew* (IRT), first appeared in 1983, but is now o/p. It offers a useful compendium of contemporary scholarship for the student. More important is Graham Stanton's own work, *A Gospel for a New People: Studies in Matthew* (T & T Clark 1991/1992 £14.95/$29.95), a volume loaded with informed and judicious comment, even where one may want to disagree. The book by R. T. France, *Matthew: Evangelist and Teacher* (/Zondervan 1989 np), is well writ-

ten and judicious on both critical and theological issues, an able introduction to the study of Matt.

One of the standard middle-level commentaries is that of *David Hill* (NCB; 1981 £9.95/$14.95). The introduction is useful, and the commentary itself is a model of compression; but its most helpful remarks are usually a digested (and not always acknowledged) form of P. Bonnard's *Evangile selon S. Matthieu* (CNT)—still one of the best treatments of Matthew for the student or pastor who can read French (esp. in the 2d ed., 1970). *W. Hendriksen* (BoT 1976 £19.95 / Baker 1973 $29.95) is verbose, preachy, and not always acquainted with current discussions, but his obvious love for Scripture and con-cern to expound the text make him a useful if stodgy guide for the preacher who will wade through him. *H. Benedict Green* (NClar; 1975 £4.95/$12.95) is very concise, and reveals an excellent knowledge of OT and rabbinic background. Although provocative and often stim-ulating, it tends toward viewpoints characterized by eccentric inde-pendence. The commentary by *C. S. Mann* and *W. F. Albright* (AB; 1971 /$30.00) is highly uneven, a poor representative of the series. They have put together a substantial introduction, but the commen-tary itself is very thin.

The spate of redaction-critical or special thematic studies on Matthew continues, a few of real value. The following is only a representative sampling of many scores of books that could be mentioned, chosen largely because they are constantly referred to in the literature and/or belong pretty closely to the commentary genre. The approaches of Bornkamm, Held, Strecker, and Trilling are summarized in J. Rohde's *Rediscovering the Teaching of the Evangelists* (o/p). At a simple level, Wolfgang Trilling (NTSR; Sheed & Ward 1978 £7.50 pb / Crossroad 1981 $4.95), a Roman Catholic scholar, attempts to combine redac-tion-critical findings on Matthew with spiritual application. *E. Schweizer* (/Westminster & John Knox 1975 $21.95) is really an extension of his Mark commentary: indeed, in this volume Schweizer devotes almost all of his space to non-Markan material in Matthew, making the work almost useless to those who do not have the other commentary. His source-critical theories and related *Sitze im Leben* are not likely to com-mand wide assent, but those theological comments that do not depend on his overarching reconstruction are often astute. *Paul Minear* (1982 o/p) has provided us with a brief redaction-critical commentary focus-ing on the structure of the book and concluding that the first gospel was originally intended as a manual for adult education in the early church. *J. D. Kingsbury,* author of a much-cited redaction-critical study of Matthew (*Matthew: Structure, Christology, Kingdom*), has written the brief (128 pp.) ProcC work (rev. ed. 1981; £8.25 pb/$8.95 pb). Few will be persuaded of the overriding importance of the Son of God title, and the work is too short to be of sustained use. Although many books on Matthew's use of the OT have appeared, the seminal one in recent discussion has been that of Krister Stendahl, *The School of St. Matthew and Its Use of the Old Testament,* and it is good to see it reprinted (/Sigler nd $24.95 hb $17.95 pb). Finally, one should perhaps mention the work of Donald Senior, *The Passion of Jesus in the Gospel of Matthew* (/Liturgical 1985 $10.95).

Old standards, a few of them recently reprinted, include *J. A. Broadus* (/Kregel 1990 [1886] $21.95 hb & $19.95 pb), which still retains some value for the preacher (although his handling of OT texts within Matthew is generally appalling), and *A. H. McNeile* on the Greek text —originally published in 1915, but now regrettably o/p. *A. Plummer* (1915 o/p) is patchy, but occasionally helpful, especially in sequences of thought. C. H. Spurgeon's exposition of Matthew bears the title *The Gospel of the Kingdom* (/Pilgrim repr. 1974 $7.95), and can be suggestive to the preacher, but it should be used only in conjunction with a modern scholarly commentary. *Joseph Addison Alexander* is again o/p. *G. H. Morrison* (/AMG, in 3 pb vols. @ $4.95) was a Scot whose 1928 exposition is on various verses in Matthew, rather than a comprehensive treatment. *David Thomas* (orig. 1873) is again o/p.

Among the shorter or more popular works, *F. V. Filson* (Black 1971 £9.99/) is only moderately useful. *R. V. G. Tasker* (TNTC; o/p) is well written but too brief to be of much value, and in any case it has now been superseded by *R. T. France*'s replacement volume for the series. *G. E. P. Cox* (TBC; o/p) suffers much from lack of space; *J. Fenton* (Pelican; 1964 £6.95/$7.95) packs more into his pages, but is very uneven in relation to the needs of the preacher. It varies from the very useful to the very disappointing. *K. Stendahl* in the New Peake uses small space with greater profit and is often worth consulting. Other popular commentaries on Matthew, all of them quite recent, include: *Myron S. Augsburger* (CC; 1987 £7.95/np), *Peter F. Ellis* (Liturgical 1986/1985 £5.50/$5.95), *Michael B. Green* (Hodder 1988 £6.95 / Word 1988 np), *Daniel J. Harrington* (/Liturgical 1986/1983 £7.50/$2.95), *Miriam Perlewitz* (MBS; Glazier 1991 £9.95 pb / Liturgical 1988 $16.95 hb & $12.95 pb), and *William G. Thompson* (Paulist 1989 £7.95/$8.95). D. A. Carson attempts to move from text to sermon in *When Jesus Confronts the World: An Exposition of Matthew 8–10* (IVP 1988 £4.25 / Baker 1987 $7.95). D. A. Carson's *God with Us* (Regal 1985 $3.95) is a brief commentary on Matthew designed for home Bible studies and adult Sunday school classes.

Past disappointments include *W. C. Allen* (ICC; 1922 £17.50/), *B. T. D. Smith* (CGT 1927 o/p), *Theodore Robinson* (Moffatt; 1947 o/p), and *J. F. Walvoord* (1974 o/p). A hybrid difficult to classify— part commentary, part expository sermon—is the work of *John MacArthur* in 4 volumes (/Moody 1985-89 @ $16.95). These books are wordy and so often betray too little time and care taken with the text that they cannot be read as reliable commentary; but the amount of information goes beyond that of most expositions. Doubtless they will well serve the well-read layperson and the poorly trained preacher.

No serious treatment of the Sermon on the Mount can afford to ignore Robert A. Guelich's *The Sermon on the Mount: A Foundation for Understanding* (/Word 1982 np), which in many respects now supersedes W. D. Davies' *The Setting of the Sermon on the Mount* (CUP 1966 £9.50/$10.95). For detailed bibliographical information on the Sermon on the Mount, we are now indebted to W. S. Kissinger's *The Sermon on the Mount: A History of Interpretation and Bibliography* (Scarecrow 1976/1975 £22.50/$26.00). Advanced studies include Hans Dieter Betz's *Essays on the Sermon on the Mount* (Fortress 1985 o/p /£23.95)—outrageously priced for 170 pp. Ostensible Greco-Roman parallels are given more weight than they deserve. More important is Georg Strecker's *The Sermon on the Mount: An Exegetical Commentary* (T & T Clark 1988 £9.95 / Abingdon 1988 $13.95). Carl G. Vaught's *The Sermon on the Mount: A Theological Interpretation* (/SUNY 1987 $44.95 hb or $14.95 pb) is worth scanning; the works by Oscar Stephen Brooks, *The Sermon on the Mount: Authentic Human Values* (UPA 1985 £19.90 hb or £8.45 pb / $37.75) and Sjef van Tilborg, *The Sermon on the Mount as an Ideological Intervention: A Reconstruction of Meaning* (Van Gorcum 1986 HFl. 65.00), in their effort to be relevant, end up domesticating the text, in service to extrabiblical ideology.

Useful popular expositions of the Sermon on the Mount include *D. M. Lloyd-Jones* (IVP 1976 £13.95 / Eerdmans 1984 $18.95); *D. A. Carson* (Paternoster 1986 £4.50 / Baker 1978 $6.95); C. H. Dodd, *Gospel and Law* (1951 o/p); *Archibald M. Hunter* (1966 o/p); J. R. W. Stott, *Christian Counter-Culture* (BST; IVP 1984 £5.75 /

IVP 1988 $11.95); *Jan Lambrecht* (Glazier 1991 £12.95 pb / Litur-
gical 1985 $12.95 pb); and Dennis Hamm, *The Beatitudes in Con-
text: What Luke and Matthew Meant* (Glazier 1991 £5.50 / Liturgical 1990 $6.95). We eagerly await the impending commentary by
Craig Blomberg in the New American Commentary series.

## 3.02 Mark

The best three all-purpose commentaries on Mark are by *C. E. B.
Cranfield* (CUP 1959 pb £15.00/), *William Lane* (NIC; 1973
/$27.95), and *C. S. Mann* (AB; 1986 /$30.00). All three are of the
highest academic standard; the first two add an attractive warmth.
Cranfield's commentary is on the Greek text; Lane's demands that
the reader know Greek only while reading the footnotes. Of the two,
Lane is slightly more conservative. Both of them are now somewhat
dated, especially the former, which was first published before the
impact of redaction-critical studies on Mark. Mann's commentary is
a major contribution. It tends, however, to focus on words and structure at the expense of theology.

The first volume by *Robert A. Guelich* (WBC on 1:1–8:26; 1989
/$24.99) is extraordinarily detailed, although sometimes incautiously
speculative. Announcements have been made of a massive (1296 pp.)
commentary on Mark by *Robert H. Gundry* (/Eerdmans 1992
$55.00), but as I have not read a line of it I cannot say anything about
it. *E. Schweizer* (/Westminster & John Knox 1970 $19.95) incorpo-
rates insight from early redactional study, sometimes with considerable profit.

Two other major commentaries, although now dated, may be mentioned. *H. B. Swete*, reprinted by /Kregel (1978 $18.95), is dated,
dull, and stodgy, in spite of its thorough scholarship. *Vincent Taylor*
(Macmillan 1966 £60.00/) was the first major commentary on Mark
in English to utilize a restrained form-criticism.

*Hugh Anderson* (NCB; rev. pb ed. 1981 £9.95/$14.95) offers a
sane presentation of Mark's theological understanding of Jesus, avoid-
ing the extreme subtleties found in some specialized recent treatments,
yet he stands painfully loose on the historical reliability of Mark. *Sher-
man Johnson* (BNTC/HNTC repr. /Hendrickson 1987 $19.95) is
disappointing in relation to the needs of the preacher. *A. M. Hunter's*
commentary is back in print (TBC; SCM 1969 £3.50 / TPI 1948
$5.95), but it does not live up to his usual standards. *C. F. D. Moule*

(CBC; 1965 £8.50 pb/$15.50 hb or $9.95 pb) packs many helpful comments into a small space, but the space is so small that the book cannot claim first priority. *Alan Cole*'s TNTC commentary has appeared in a revised edition (1990 £4.75 / 1989 $8.95). It is certainly worth careful reading, but cannot compete with Lane and Cranfield. *C. L. Mitton* (Epworth 1957 o/p) offers the preacher many practical and helpful points but is both dated and hard to come by. *Dennis E. Nineham* (Pelican; 1969/1964 £6.99/$7.95) is stimulating, but occasionally irritating owing to a penchant to read behind the passage rather than the passage, and sometimes in defiance of the passage. *Larry Hurtado*'s 1983 GNC commentary has metamorphosed into its NIBC form (1989 $9.95). It is a moderately redaction-critical commentary that will serve pastors well when used in conjunction with Lane or Cranfield.

Among older works, *A. E. J. Rawlinson* (o/p) can sometimes be picked up s/h. *Joseph Alexander* is still in print (/Kregel nd $17.95).

Useful tools include R. P. Martin's *Mark: Evangelist and Theologian* (Paternoster 1979 £6.50 / Zondervan 1986 $10.95), which is not a commentary but a useful study of the background and theology of Mark as treated in contemporary scholarship; Hugh M. Humphrey's *A Bibliography for the Gospel of Mark: 1954–1980* (Mellen 1989/1982 £29.95/$49.95); and Frank J. Matera's *What Are They Saying about Mark?* (Paulist 1987 £4.95/$4.95). Etienne Trocmé's *The Formation of the Gospel according to Mark* (1975 o/p) is not really a commentary, but an exposition of Trocmé's mildly eccentric but always stimulating views on the Gospel's development. Two other recent works that are not commentaries but that contribute substantially to our understanding are Martin Hengel's *Studies in the Gospel of Mark* (SCM/ 1985 £8.50), and Ernest Best's *Mark: The Gospel as Story* (T & T Clark 1988 £8.95 pb / Books International 1989 $19.95 pb). Bas van Iersel's *Reading Mark* (T & T Clark/Liturgical 1989 £9.95/$14.95), the ET of a work that originally appeared in Dutch, makes literary criticism comprehensible to the general reader. It includes many useful insights, and is worth a good, fast, read. M. D. Hooker's *The Message of Mark* (Epworth/TPI 1983 £4.95/$7.95) covers much in few words.

*W. Hendriksen* on Mark (BoT 1976 £15.95 / Baker 1975 $19.95) is not as good as on Matthew. *Walter W. Wessel* (EBC vol.8, bound with Matthew) makes reasonable use of small space, but without much interaction with secondary literature. Now in a revised edition, *P. J.*

*Achtemeier* (ProcC; 1987/1986 £8.25 pb/$8.95 pb) makes too much of the church crisis in the 60s A.D., and too little of the historical Jesus.

Among the more popular treatments, *Johnnie C. Godwin* (LBBC; 1979 $7.50), *Terence J. Keegan* (Paulist 1981 £6.95/), *John J. Kilgallen* (Paulist 1989 /$14.95), and *Ralph Martin* (KPG; 1986/1981 £3.95/$5.95) are responsible surveys of their kind. *R. Kent Hughes* (/Crossway 1989 2 vols. @ $13.95) is more sermonic, but one of the best in that genre. Other popular treatments include *Karen A. Barta* (MBS; 1991/1988 £6.95 pb/$13.95 hb or $8.95 pb), *Paul R. McReynolds* (/Standard 1989 $9.95), Ivor Powell (/Kregel 1986 $19.95), and *Michael Wilcock* (/CLC 1983 $4.95). The book by Frederick Neumann, *The Binding Truth: A Selective Homiletical Commentary on the New Testament*, vol. 2: *Why Are You Afraid? The Gospels of Mark and John* (/Pickwick 1984 np) is so odd I am uncertain why it was published. Neumann died in 1967. This is posthumously published sermonic material, with useful nuggets but no structure and an English style that is not easy to read.

### 3.03 Luke

The most comprehensive commentary in English is that of *Joseph A. Fitzmyer* (AB; 2 vols. 1981 & 1985 /$40.00). The work is a masterpiece of learning, and written with clarity and verve. Not all will be persuaded by the author's positions on dating, sources, and details of historicity, but there are few questions Fitzmyer has not thought deeply about, and his competence in the Semitic parallels informs his work throughout. No less learned is the large commentary by *I. Howard Marshall* (NIGTC 1978 £27.25 hb & £19.95 pb/$37.50 hb). Unfortunately the prose is so densely packed, owing not least to the fact that the notes are incorporated into the text, that some will make heavy weather of it. Moreover it presupposes reasonable proficiency in the Greek text. Those with the requisite skills will benefit greatly from reading it.

In the same sort of category, although harder to assess because it is still incomplete, is the commentary by *John Nolland* (WBC), the first volume of which covers 1:1–9:20 (1989 /$24.99). Another major commentary (933 pp.) is the recent work of *C. F. Evans* (TPINT; 1990 $39.95). Theologically it stands in a far more skeptical tradition than either Marshall or Fitzmyer, and rarely interacts with literature and positions of a more centrist (let alone conservative) stance. *Luke*

*Timothy Johnson* (SacPag; 1992 /$29.95) is above all a work of literary analysis. It tends not to take up issues of, say, the origin of a pericope, or development of ideas or tradition before the text as it stands. It devotes quite a bit of space to literary analogies in the ancient world. Robert C. Tannehill, *The Narrative Unity of Luke–Acts: A Literary Interpretation*, vol. 1: *The Gospel According to Luke* (Fortress 1987 £18.50/$24.95), writes with similar interests at heart. *David L. Tiede* (ACNT; 1988 /$19.95) is a nontechnical commentary that adopts more or less standard positions. Written in a condensed style, this commentary assumes that most of Luke's stances reflect considerably later Christianity rather than its ostensible subject. The commentary by *David Gooding* (IVP/Eerdmans 1987 £7.50 / o/p) focuses attention on the text, especially its flow, but does not interact with other literature. It is a fine way for the serious general reader to get into the text of Luke.

*E. E. Ellis* (NCB; 1981 £8.95 / o/p) contains valuable material especially on the background and purposes of passages and on the flow of the argument, but can be thin on particular verses. Similarly, *G. B. Caird* (Pelican; Penguin/Viking Penguin 1990/1964 £5.99/$7.95) is good value for money, although comments can be thin on the details. The series aim is not to provide material that is technical or devotional but simply "to bring out the meaning the Evangelists intended to convey to their original readers." *A. R. C. Leaney* (BNTC; Black 1985 £10.95 / Hendrickson 1987 $19.95) tends to be thin where one most hopes for help. *J. M. Creed* (Macmillan 1942 o/p) is better, but decisively belongs to prewar scholarship. *G. H. P. Thompson* (NClar 1972 £4.95 / o/p) is a moderately useful and fairly conservative commentary, but it is severely restricted by lack of space. *A. Plummer* (ICC; 4th ed. 1901 £19.95/$29.95) was once good, but its reputation lingers on after later writers have superseded the work. *W. Manson* did himself less than justice in the Moffatt series (1930 o/p). *E. Tinsley* (CBC; 1965 £8.95/$13.95) is occasionally useful over and above the larger commentaries, but skip it unless the book can be borrowed. F. Danker's *Jesus and the New Age According to St Luke* (Fortress 1987 £18.50/$21.95) is of some value to the scholar and the layperson, but the heart of his argument reappears in his little ProcC work (1987 /$8.95). *W. R. F. Browning* (TBC; 1982 o/p) is surprisingly good, but too brief to be of primary importance. *Leon Morris* (TNTC; rev. ed. 1988 £4.95/$9.95) is excellent value for money, one of the better volumes in the series—even if occasionally the constraints of the series means he skates over some difficult questions and skirts some contemporary issues rather easily. *R. Summers* (/Word 1972) and *W. J. Harrington* (/Newman 1967) are both o/p. *Michael Wilcock* (BST; 2d ed. 1984 £5.75/$11.95) provides some excellent grist for the preacher's mill, provided he is used in conjunction with a major commentary. *Walter L. Liefeld* (EBC vol. 8, bound with Matthew and Mark) packs a great deal of astute comment into relatively small compass. In still smaller compass but with less astuteness, *Robert J. Karris* (/Doubleday 1977 $3.95) offers a brief commentary based on the Jerusalem Bible. *Robert E. Obach* and *Albert Kirk* (Paulist 1986 £7.95/$8.95) is worth a glance, as is *Philip van Linden* (MBS; 1991/1986 £6.95 pb/$12.95 hb or $8.95 pb). *Lewis Foster* (/Standard 1986 $12.95) is not worth even that. R. E. O. White's *Luke's Case for Christianity* (Bible Reading Fellowship 1987 £2.75 / Morehouse 1990 $6.95) is the sort of thing to put into the hand of the layperson just beginning to do some serious Bible reading.

From the preacher's point of view, *J. Norval Geldenhuys* (NIC; 1951 /$27.95) is still worth skimming, together with the old two-volume commentary by *F. Godet* (T & T Clark 2 vols. nd, vol. 1 /$39.95, no info on vol. 2 /Kregel repr. 1982 in 1 vol. £19.95/). Godet is virtually precritical, but can be valuable. Apart from his digressions on old and forgotten controversies, he is consistently clear and to the point. He is still worth using in conjunction with a more modern work. Useful in the same sorts of ways is *William Hendriksen* (NTC; 1979/1978 £19.95/$29.95).

Useful reprints include *William Kelly* (/Kregel nd $19.95), and *G. H. Morison*, 2 vols. (/AMG 1979 @ $4.95). *Fred Craddock* in the Interpretation series (/Westminster & John Knox 1990 $21.95) is interesting precisely because Craddock is a fine homiletician. His book is more in the form of expository essays than of commentary. Charles H. Talbert, *Reading Luke: A New Commentary for Preachers* [=British subtitle; American subtitle, *A Literary and Theological Commentary on the Third Gospel*] (SPCK 1990 £9.99 /Crossroad 1984 $13.95) focuses on movement of thought, but as a result somehow dilutes the connection with the historical Jesus.

If I were to mention the numerous works that are not commentaries but that nevertheless contribute substantially to understanding the text, this little book would immediately quadruple in size, so in general I refrain. Nevertheless there are a few works that should be mentioned. Bo Reicke's *The Gospel of Luke* (/John Knox 1964 o/p) is not strictly a commentary, but can be seminal in sermon preparation. I. Howard Marshall's *Luke: Historian and Theologian* (/Zondervan repr. 1989 [1971] $13.95) is an admirable study, similar to France on Matthew, but of course much more dated. Serious students of Luke–Acts may want to read the collection of essays edited by Leander E. Keck and J. Louis Martyn, *Studies in Luke-Acts* (/Fortress 1980 o/p), a work that depicted just where the center of contemporary debate on this corpus was a decade and a half ago. A more popular but more recent book of the same kind is Mark Allan Power's *What Are They Saying About Luke?* (Paulist 1989 £4.95/$5.95). Charles H. Talbert's *Literary Patterns, Theological Themes and the Genre of Luke–Acts* (SBLMS 20; /SP 1974 $42.00) argues that Luke's compositional procedure is akin to steps taken in Suetonius's *Life of Virgil*, Pliny's *Letters*, and Lucian's *How to Write History*, merged with the pastoral model of Paul's letters. It is not clear that Talbert has learned from the severe criticism levelled at his earlier book on the genre of the Gospels (especially by David E. Aune), but the fruit of this study resurfaces in Talbert's *Reading Luke*, already listed. One might also mention Robert J. Karris's *Luke: Artist and Theologian: Luke's Passion Account as Literature* (Paulist 1985 £6.95 / o/p), an important study, and S. G. Wilson's *Luke and the Law* (SNTSMS 50; CUP 1983/1984 £27.50/$32.50)—although I do not find his thesis convincing. Jan Wojcik's *The Road to Emmaus: Reading Luke's Gospel* (/Purdue University Press 1989 $21.50) is poorly written, and more interested in literary categories and psychological impact than in what Luke actually says. It is too clever by half. One very useful volume is Joseph A. Fitzmyer's *Luke the Theologian: Aspects of his Teaching* (Paulist 1989 £12.95/$11.95).

## 3.04 John

Probably no major book of the NT has been served by more commentaries during the last few decades than this one. At least a couple of dozen of these are extremely light, and of these lighter contributions only a sampling can be included here.

Among the major works on John, the best one-volume treatment of the Greek text is that of *C. K. Barrett*, in the revised edition (SPCK/Westminster 1978 £30.00/$28.95). Although Barrett stands needlessly free from John's historical claims, especially in the passion narrative (cf., for instance, Shwerwin-White on the trial), neverthe-less this work is not only elegantly and lucidly written, it is usually pro-found in its grasp of John's theological message, and rightly skeptical about many modern literary and historical reconstructions. *Leon Morris*(NIC; 1970 /$29.95) is an encyclopedic treatment from the strictly "earthly-historical" view of Jesus' ministry. This is one of the major conservative commentaries on John, and its footnotes are a mine of quotable material. Sometimes the style is choppy, and there are numer-ous theological and historical questions that are not probed very deeply. The predecessor to Morris's work in the NIC series, by *Merrill C. Tenney*, has not been superseded by Tenney's contribution to EBC (vol.9 bound with Acts; 1981 \$28.95). Unfortunately this lat-ter treatment is so thin, dated, and sometimes even naive that it can safely be given a miss. It may provide interesting suggestions to the unsophisticated Sunday school teacher. Two more recent commen-taries that lay claim to the evangelical tradition are by *George R. Beasley-Murray* (WBC; 1987 /$24.99) and *D. A. Carson* (IVP/Eerdmans 1991 £19.95/$29.95). The former is rather thin for the first two-thirds of the Gospel, and then becomes very rich indeed, especially in the passion narrative. Some readers will be less than convinced by the source-critical "solution" to the challenges of chapter 20. Carson's work is rather more difficult for me to assess.

Other recent commentaries on the Gospel of John are: Peter F. Ellis's *The Genius of John: A Composition-Critical Commentary on the Fourth Gospel* (Liturgical 1986/1984 £9.75/$10.95), *G. S. Sloyan* in the Interpretation series (/Westminster & John Knox 1987 $19.95), and *Kenneth Grayston* (Epworth 1990 £7.50 / [in the U.S. ed. belonging to a new "Narrative Commentaries" series] TPI 1990 $14.95). None is substantial enough to compete with the major com-mentaries. Ellis and Grayston sometimes provide insight into the movement of thought in the text. All three are overly skeptical about John's witness to history.

*R. E. Brown* (AB; 2 vols.; G. Chapman 1971 @ £29.95 / Dou-bleday 1966 & 1970, $25.00 & $24.00 respectively) is crystal clear and very useful. At one time it was especially useful to the student, because of its extensive bibliography, but this is now dated. The work's notes and cross-references are a mine of information; for the same rea-son the sheer volume of material may discourage the reader in a hurry. It is one of the best contributions in the AB series, and is a fine rep-resentative of moderate NT Roman Catholic scholarship. That does not mean that his five stages of literary development, or the sacramentalism he finds running through the text, will command assent among all interpreters. In some ways, Brown's work has been superseded by *R. Schnackenburg* (3 vols.; ET 1980–82 Burns & Oates £80 the set, vol. prices £35.00, £25.00, £30.00 / Crossroad 1990 pb @ $19.95; the German original has a fourth vol. of updating and explanatory essays, 1984), whose allegiance to Roman Catholic tradition is combined with shrewdness, some pastoral concern, and a moderate critical stance. Now severely dated, the ET of the contribution by *Rudolf Bultmann* (/Westminster & John Knox 1971 $26.50) is still a provocative classic of continental scholarship, but not very helpful to the preacher. *Barnabas Lindars* (NCB pb ed. 1981 £12.95 / o/p) is a model of concise writing, offering its own solution to the development of the Fourth Gospel in a theory of developing sermon notes; but it cannot compete with the longer works, and it is sometimes pretty dry. W. Hendriksen (BoT 1959 £17.95 / Baker 1961 $24.95), apart from being dated, may be of some value to the preacher, but with the weaknesses inherent in the series already noted in this book. The ET of the posthumously published commentary by *Ernst Haenchen* has appeared in two volumes (Hermeneia 1984 @ £26.50/$35.95). This is a major disappointment. Despite the best editorial efforts of Ulrich Busse, Haenchen's student, and of the translator and English editor, Robert W. Funk, the fact remains that the scholarship is terribly dated, and thinner and thinner as one progresses through the Gospel. In the latter half, entire pericopae may be summed up in a few lines of comment. Bibliography is slanted, uneven, and dated. The work may be an interesting insight into Haenchen's mind and scholarship in the closing years of his life, but it is a shame to allot the space in so prestigious a series to a half-finished and obsolete contribution.

The BNTC/HNTC contribution by *J. N. Sanders* and *B. A. Mastin*, orig. 1968, has come back into print (Black 1985 £10.99 pb / Hendrickson 1987 $19.95 pb). *John Marsh* (Pelican; 1971/1968 £6.99 pb/$8.95 pb) offers comments that are sometimes suggestive and fresh, but too frequently uneven. *R. V. G. Tasker* (TNTC repr. 1983 [1960] £4.50/$8.95) is brief and to the point, but now so severely dated as not to be on anyone's list of priorities.

*J. H. Bernard* (ICC; 1923 2 vols. @ £17.50/$29.95) writes with all the individuality, if not eccentricity, which some might expect from an Irish archbishop. The work is thoroughly uneven, occasionally good. Among other reprints of older works are *E. W. Hengstenberg* (2 vols. /Kregel nd $36.95); *Alfred Plummer* (again o/p); and *David Thomas* (2 vols. in 1 /Kregel 1980 [1885] $24.95). *William H. van Doren* (again o/p, orig. 1872) is in some ways a strange work. Its endless stream of "one-liners" can be suggestive to preachers who have done their exegesis before picking up this book. In a class by itself is the critical translation, by Fabian R. Larcher, of *Thomas Aquinas* (/Magi 1980 $35.00). This commentary varies from the good to the masterful. It is always worth consulting, even if on critical issues it is of course hopelessly dated. The thoughtful reader will always discern practical applications if he or she ponders the remarks of *F. Godet* (2 vols. in 1 /Kregel 1980 [1885] £19.95/$36.95). Both of *B. F. Westcott*'s two commentaries, one on the Greek text and the other on the English, are now regrettably o/p. If they are disappointing this is because they have been thoroughly picked over by later scholars. Westcott offers thorough exegesis with hints at applications that are there for the discerning reader, but the reputation of the commentaries grew when there was little better. His works are worth consulting but hardly the first priority.

*Marcus Dods* (not to be confused with C. H. Dodd!) wrote the commentaries both in the EGNT series (the entire 5-vol. set, ed. W. Robertson Nicoll, is still available from /Eerdmans 1952 $89.95) and in the EB series (2 vols. o/p). Dods is old and semiliberal, but often suggestive and practical. *G. H. MacGregor* (Moffatt; 1928 o/p) is disappointingly colorless. *Alan Richardson* (TBC; 1964 o/p) is not at his best on John and fails to live up to the standard he achieves in other writings. *A. M. Hunter*'s small commentary (CBC; 1965 £9.50 pb/$13.95 pb) is much more useful. *J. C. Fenton* (NClar; 1979 o/p) and *W. E. Hull* (Broadman; vol. 9, bound with M. D. Tolbert on Luke 1970 /$19.95 [/$225.00 the set]) are both too brief to be of great help. *D. M. Smith* has written the ProcC contribution (1986 /$8.95), a 128-pp. collection of nine essays that constitute less of a commentary (although John 1, 9, and 16 receive closer attention) than a penetrating summary presentation of the current state of Johannine scholarship.

By far the best of the "popular" commentaries is that of *F. F. Bruce* (Pickering 1983 £8.95 pb / Eerdmans 1984 $18.95). This provides a straightforward exposition in 424 pp. of the text as it stands, with virtually no consideration of critical problems (although the alert reader will often detect the sagacity that has gone into critical deci-

sions before pen touched paper). Written about the same level is the
very useful volume by *Robert Kysar* (ACNT; 1986 /$16.95). A few
other popular works may be mentioned, but most of these are not
worth a great deal of time: *George W. Macrae* (/Doubleday 1978
$2.95); *Lesslie Newbigin* (1982 o/p); *Robert E. Obach* and *Albert Kirk*
(Paulist 1979 £6.95 / 1981 $7.95). Two slim volumes by Robert
Kysar, *John the Maverick Gospel* (/Westminster & John Knox
1986/1976 £6.95/$9.95) and *John's Story of Jesus* (/Augsburg-
Fortress 1984 £4.50/$6.95), add little to his more important ACNT
volume. The book by *Fred B. Craddock* (KPG; 1986 £4.95 / 1987
$6.95) has its interest because of Craddock's skill as a homiletician.
The work by *Thomas E. Crane* (/Alba 1980 $5.95 pb) is less a com-
mentary on the Fourth Gospel than a popular exposition of John, 1
John, and Revelation, to emphasize how John interprets his own expe-
rience of knowing God. The book is steeped in Roman Catholic tradition. The same is true of *John Wijngaards* (MBS; 1991 £9.95 pb /
1986 $16.95 hb or $12.95 pb), who adopts a critical stance akin to
Brown or Schnackenburg, frequently finds "mysticism" in the text,
and is much interested in the community behind the text. Raymond
Brown's *The Gospel and Epistles of John: A Concise Commentary* [and
thus not to be confused with his AB volumes] (Liturgical 1988
£3.95/$3.95) is so brief (136 pp.) it can be given a miss. In addition
to his NCB commentary, *Barnabas Lindars* has also produced the
"New Testament Guides" volume on John (JSOT 1990 £4.95/$7.95).
The slim volume by Donald Guthrie, *Exploring God's Word: A Guide
to John's Gospel* (1986 o/p), is very thin indeed, but the inductive
approach might help some laypersons in their personal Bible study, if
you can get hold of a copy. *John G. Mitchell* (1982 $13.95) is wordy,
based on the KJV (it does not even raise the text-critical questions at
5:3 and 7:59–8:11), and not particularly reliable. The four-volume
set of expositions by Leon Morris, *Reflections on the Gospel of John*
(/Baker 1986–89 @ $8.95, or $34.95 the set), will help laypersons,
and might give some preachers some ideas about how to move from
text to people, but should not displace Morris's commentary.

Before leaving John, perhaps I should mention a few of the myri-
ads of special studies on this Gospel. William Temple's *Readings in
St John's Gospel* (Macmillan 1961 £13.99 / Morehouse 1985 $8.95)
is a minor classic, full of down-to-earth application of (mostly) Johannine themes, although its hermeneutics is sometimes dubious. C. H.
Dodd's *The Interpretation of the Fourth Gospel* (CUP 1968 £22.50

pb/$22.95 pb) defends the thesis that the closest parallel to John is the Hellenistic world of the Hermetic writings—a viewpoint few will defend today. Nevertheless the book remains useful on broader themes and approaches. Leon Morris's *Studies in the Fourth Gospel* (1969 o/p) is still useful for some of its thematic studies; its essays on criticism have largely been superseded by the introduction in Carson's commentary. But Morris's *Jesus is the Christ: Studies in the Theology of John* (IVP 1989 £8.95 / Eerdmans 1989 $12.95) includes some really excellent theological essays, and is well worth the price. Although it does not attempt a systematic exposition of Johannine themes, it is more interesting and stimulating than G. R. Beasley-Murray's *John: Word Biblical Themes* (/Word 1989 np); Daniel J. Harrington's *John's Thought and Theology: An Introduction* (Glazier 1991/1990 £8.50/$8.95); John Ashton's (ed.) *The Interpretation of John* (IRT; 1988 o/p); or John Fenton's *Finding the Way through John* (Mowbray 1988 £6.95/)—really a slender "running paragraph" commentary of 105 pp. Two useful surveys of contemporary scholarship on John are those of Stephen Smalley, *John—Evangelist and Interpreter* (Paternoster 1983 £6.95 / o/p), and Robert Kysar, *The Fourth Evangelist and His Gospel* (/Augsburg 1975 o/p). Cutting his own thoughtful swath through the secondary literature, D. Moody Smith, *Johannine Christianity: Essays on its Setting, Sources, and Theology* (/University of South Carolina Press 1989 $13.95 pb), sets a standard in careful style and reflection, even though not all will agree with his conclusions. John Ashton's *Understanding the Fourth Gospel* (OUP 1991 £69.00/$139.00) is outrageously priced (even for a book of 550 pp.), but an elegantly written and important volume for the more advanced student. Ashton, a student of Xavier Léon-Dufour, largely focuses on Bultmann, wanting to take what is best from him while avoiding his radicalism, a-temporal theology, individualism, and abstraction from historical questions. There are some good treatments of individual themes. The book would have been extraordinarily important if it had been published twenty-five years ago, when the influence of Bultmann was ubiquitous. Paul S. Minear's *John: The Martyr's Gospel* (/Pilgrim 1985 $8.95) is analogous to his work on Matthew. R. Alan Culpepper's *Anatomy of the Fourth Gospel: A Study in Literary Design* (Fortress 1987 £13.75 pb/$14.95) applies the new literary criticism to John, and offers many fresh insights. At the same time, his adoption of the nineteenth-century novel as his controlling paradigm leads to not a few anomalies. Finally, my own *The Farewell*

*Discourse and Final Prayer of Jesus* [=US title; British title is *Jesus and His Friends*] (IVP 1986 £4.95 / Baker 1981 $7.95) is an exposition of John 14–17. My book *Divine Sovereignty and Human Responsibility* (1981) explores the theme suggested by the title in the Fourth Gospel against Jewish background, but this work is more technical and presupposes a basic theological education. It is in any case o/p, although the publisher is now talking about bringing it back.

## 3.05 Acts

The Book of Acts is still not particularly well served by commentaries. *E. Haenchen* (Blackwell 1982 £25.00 / Westminster & John Knox 1971 $29.95) is important for the really serious student, but its deviously complex reconstructions of Luke's sources and theological interests, not infrequently in defiance of hard evidence, makes it an unsuitable starting-point for most preachers. The standard critical commentary is probably now that of *H. Conzelmann* (Hermeneia; 1987 £30.00/$39.95), but it is tied far too tightly to a modified history-of-religions approach. The source- and redaction-critical interests of Gerd Lüdemann's *Early Christianity According to the Traditions in Acts: A Commentary* (SCM/Fortress 1989 £15.00/$19.95) are everywhere apparent. *F. F. Bruce* has written two commentaries on Acts. The one in the NL/NIC series (o/p /Eerdmans np) is generally more useful to the preacher, although the one published earlier on the Greek text, and recently revised and enlarged (IVP 1991 £22.95 / Eerdmans 1990 $39.95) offers substantial technical information. Neither commentary is trite or obvious, but one might have been glad of more theology. Very useful is the TNTC contribution by *I. Howard Marshall* (1983 £4.95 / 1980 $9.95), who was apparently given more space than the constraints of that series normally allow. This is the replacement for *E. M. Blaiklock* (o/p) who is amazingly thin on theology, for which coins and inscriptions are no substitute. Quite excellent is the EBC commentary by *Richard N. Longenecker* (bound with John; Hodder 1987 £22.50 / Zondervan 1986 $28.95)—one of the best in the series. Not quite as good, but well worth reading, are *David John Williams* (GNC; metamorphosed into its NIBC form, /$9.95), and *G. A. Krodel* (ACNT; 1986 /$8.95 pb). The commentary by *French L. Arrington* (/Hendrickson 1988 $16.95) is not theologically rich, but generally useful, if one overlooks the occasionally intrusive semi-Pelagianism.

*Johannes Munck* (AB; 1967 /$20.00 pb) has nothing of the sparkle of his *Paul and the Salvation of Mankind*, and is frankly disappointing. *Foakes-Jackson* (1931 o/p) is quite abysmal, and it has been suggested that he spent all his inspiration on the monumental classic that he edited, together with Kirsopp Lake, *The Beginnings of Christianity* (5 vols.; recently repr. by Baker, but again o/p).

The preacher may still find help in the turn-of-the-century work by *R. B. Rackham* (o/p). Rackham was a devout high churchman, shrewd in his practical comments. He rightly calls attention to a theology of the church, but does so with restraint. The complementary emphasis on witness and mission is stressed by C. F. D. Moule in *Christ's Messengers* (o/p), which is a study (not a commentary) of the first part of Acts, and very briefly by *R. R. Williams* (TBC; 1965 o/p). Useful all-round commentaries have been produced by *C. S. C. Williams* (BNTC/HNTC; /Hendrickson 1987 [1957] $19.95) and, more recently, *W. H. Willimon* (Interpretation; /Westminster & John Knox 1988 $17.95), but Longenecker and Marshall are better. As a practical supplement *J. Alexander*'s commentary (BoT 1980 £14.50/$29.95) suggests various lines of thought. *W. Neil* (NCB; 1982 £8.95 / 1981 $12.95) is too brief to give much help where it is most needed. *E. F. Harrison* (/Zondervan 1986 $15.95) was dated before it appeared. Doubtless it would be useful to the general reader. *G. A. Krodel* in the ProcC series (1985 £4.50 / 1981 $8.95) is too brief to serve as more than a quick supplement, and in any case it has been superseded by his own ACNT volume, already listed. *Lloyd C. Ogilvie* (CC; 1983 np) contains useful material, but is sometimes more interested in communication than in a careful understanding of the material to be communicated. *Charles H. Talbert* (KPG; 1984 /$6.95) is too thin to be of great use. *John R. W. Stott*'s work on Acts is one of the best in the BST series (IVP/ 1990). Numerous thin expositions flood the market, but need take up no space on the preacher's shelf.

Five studies should be mentioned. Invaluable for the serious student is W. W. Gasque's *A History of the Criticism of the Acts of the Apostles*, recently reprinted (/Hendrickson 1985 $14.95 pb). Briefer and a firm critique of the more speculative wing of scholarship on Acts is Martin Hengel's *Acts and the History of Earliest Christianity* (SCM 1986 £10.50 / o/p). The posthumously published work of Colin J. Hemer, *The Book of Acts in the Setting of Hellenistic History* (WUNT; Mohr-Siebeck 1989 DM 128 / Coronet 1989 $88.50), is a wonderfully erudite study of the social context of Acts, with countless insights and careful bridling of theological interpretations that leave the controls of history behind, but its price will put it out of the hands of most students and preachers. Read it in a good library. Not nearly so controlled is Jerome Neyrey, ed., *The Social World of Luke–Acts: Models for Interpretation* (/Hendrickson 1991 $19.95), which sometimes confuses carefully examined social context with comparatively uncontrolled modern social theory. The work by Robert C. Tannehill, *The Narrative Unity of Luke Acts: A Literary Interpretation*, 2 vols.: *The Acts of the Apostles* (Fortress 1990 £24.95/$26.95) is the companion volume to Tannehill's study of Luke, already mentioned.

## 3.06 Romans

Probably the best Romans commentary now available is still the new ICC work by *C. E. B. Cranfield* (2 vols. 1975–79; @ £19.95/$39.95). Occasionally Cranfield seems more influenced by Barth than by Paul, but for thoughtful exegesis of the Greek text, with a careful weighing of alternative positions, there is nothing quite like it. An abbreviated (320 pp.) edition is also available that makes fewer demands on the reader (T & T Clark/Eerdmans 1985 £12.95/$15.95 pb). The two-volume work by *James D. G. Dunn* (WBC; 1988 @ /$24.99) is of course more up-to-date bibliographically, and is certainly worthy of diligent study. Nevertheless one of its controlling foci, namely, the thesis that Paul and his readers are wrestling over the signs of membership in the people of God, is rather overdone, and is in general too indebted to E. P. Sanders. Another recent and major commentary is the work by *John Ziesler* (TPINT; 1989 £9.50 pb/$24.95), who writes with clarity and frequently takes independent stances that provoke reflection. *Douglas Moo*'s first volume (WEC; on Romans 1–8; 1991 np), almost 600 pp. long, has a very thin introduction, but thoughtfully interacts with the best of the secondary literature in the commentary itself, and works conscientiously through the text. Moo adopts more traditional interpretations of such categories as justification, but plows fairly independent furrows here and there (e.g., in his interpretation of Rom. 7). The series to which it belongs has been cancelled by the publisher. Most of the volumes in preparation are being taken over by Baker, but Moo's work will be reformatted to NIC style, and his second volume, bound with the revision of his first, will eventually appear from Eerdmans as the NIC volume that replaces *John Murray*. Moo's commentary promises to become a standard. *E. Käsemann* is available in ET (/Eerdmans 1978 $25.95). Käsemann is brilliant and infuriating, alternating theologically between the insightful and the tradition-bound (he writes in the modern Lutheran tradition, although for political reasons he is a member of the German Methodist Church). No one who reads him can remain neutral about anything he says.

Numerous other helpful commentaries on Romans are available. One of the best for the theological sequence of thought in Romans is the work of *Anders Nygren* (Fortress 1949 £8.25 pb/$10.95 pb). Everyone who can do so should grasp his general introductory remarks on pp.16–26. Unfortunately, however, the book is inadequate as a verse-by-verse commentary. Here, apart from those mentioned, one might profitably turn to *F. J. Leenhardt* (1961; regrettablyt o/p) or *C. K. Barrett* (BNTC/HNTC; 1957 £14.99 pb/). The latter is good, but not quite as memorable as Barrett's two commentaries on the Corinthian correspondence. Nygren, Leenhardt, and Barrett complement each other admirably. *Karl Barth*'s inspiring earlier commentary (6th ed. OUP 1969 £10.95 / Peter Smith 1991 $21.95) is still available. Sometimes Barth comes closer to Kierkegaard than to Paul, but almost anything can be forgiven when Barth shows he has grasped, like Nygren, the heart of this epistle—or, rather, like Nygren, that he has been grasped by it. Everyone ought to sample it (e.g., on 3:1ff.). In the same tradition of Lutheran scholarship as Barth, Nygren, and Käsemann, but at a lighter level, is *Roy A. Harrisville* (ACNT; 1980 /$13.95). Not worth more than a quick skim are *P. J. Achtemeier* (Interpretation; John Knox 1986/1985 £12.95/$19.95) and *John Paul Heil* (Paulist 1987 £8.95/$9.95). Brendan Byrne, *Reckoning with Romans: A Contemporary Reading of Paul's Gospel* (Glazier 1991 £9.95 / Liturgical 1986 $12.95) is surprisingly good. One raises eyebrows here and there, but many old truths are set out in fresh ways. The forty theses at the end of the book are worth pondering. *Leon Morris* (IVP/Eerdmans 1988 £15.95/$29.95) has produced a workmanlike commentary in traditional mold. Its strength is the seriousness with which it takes the text; its weakness is its failure to grapple with the tenor of Pauline studies since E. P. Sanders (on which more below). *Ernest F. Scott* has been reprinted (Greenwood 1979 [1947] £32.50/$38.50).

In the revised edition, *F. F. Bruce* (TNTC; 1986/1985 £4.50/$8.95) repays study, but the work was not as extensively revised as one might have wished. *W. Sanday* and *A. C. Headlam* (ICC; 1902 £19.95/$29.95) are not as dull as is often supposed. *John Murray* (NIC; 1960 /$29.95) will guide you stolidly with the heavy tread of the proverbial village policeman (although with more theology; and note especially the useful appendices and notes); while at the other end of the scale *H. C. G. Moule* (EB; o/p) will fill your soul with lovely thoughts, even if you have something less tangible at the end than you expected. Oddly enough Moule is better in the CBSC series (/CLC repr. 1975 [1899] $4.95 pb).

*C. H. Dodd*'s commentary (Moffatt; 1932 o/p) has been described as a classic, although on many passages it is hard to see why. He consistently flattens future tenses into present ones, and pushes his own theories at the reader. *T. W. Manson* offers concise but useful comments in the New Peake; *A. M. Hunter* (TBC; 1968 o/p) sketches some helpful themes. But both are too brief to compete with the heavyweights. *John Knox* provides a significant commentary in IB (vol. 9 binds Acts & Romans; 1977/1954 £21.50 for the volume / $324.95 the set) but he has a blind spot about the basis of Pauline ethics. *J. C. O'Neill* (Pelican; o/p) is so eccentric in his source theories (Paul did not write about one-third of Romans) that this is unlikely to be the first commentary to which students and preachers will turn. *M. Black* (NCB; 1989 £5.99/$13.95) has some strong points, but is not a first choice. *E. F. Harrison* (EBC vol. 10, bound with Corinthians and Galatians; 1976 /$28.95) is responsible in his comments, but provides little interaction and not much spark. *W. Hendriksen* (NTC 2 vols.; vol. 1 1980 £6.95 hb; vol. 2 1981 £5.95 hb; 2 vols. in one 1982 13.95 / $24.95) some find helpful; from that tradition, Murray is to be preferred. *Ernest Best* (CBC; 1967 £8.50 pb/$12.95 pb) does not live up to his work elsewhere, doubtless owing in large part to the constraints of the series.

There are many popular-level treatments of Romans, most of which will not be noticed here, and a few choice reprints. *F. L. Godet* (Kregel 1982/1991 £19.95/$24.95 hb or $18.95 pb) is not at his best on Rom., but still worth skimming. *Charles Hodge* (BoT 1989/1975 £8.95/$17.95) has been eclipsed by Murray. In some ways the reprint of *Robert Haldane* (/Kregel nd $30.95 hb or $24.95 pb) is more important. *Hermann Olshausen* (/Kregel nd $17.95) sometimes offers independent interpretations that are worth pondering. John R. W. Stott in *Men Made New* (/Baker repr. 1984 [1966] $5.95) provides a first-class exposition of chapters 5–8, whether or not one finally agrees with, say, his treatment of Romans 7. As well as being directly practical, he firmly grasps nettles of theological interpretation. The ten volumes of *D. Martyn Lloyd-Jones*'s exposition (9 vols., not published in sequential order, but covering 1:1–8:39, are available from BoT/ Zondervan 1970-1989, prices ranging per vol. £8.95–£12.95/ $12.95–$17.95 or the set for $143.60; vol. 10., on Romans 9, seems to be available only from BoT/ 1991 £12.95) is probably not the model most preachers should imitate, but the set is easy to read, and Lloyd-Jones sometimes offers material one is hard pressed to find elsewhere—in addition to the wealth of his practical application of Scripture. In shorter compass is James Philip's *The Power of God: An Exposition of Paul's Letter to the Romans* (N. Gray 1987 £4.95 pb/). I have not in general mentioned brief study guides, but I cannot forbear to mention *R. Bower* (SPCK/ 1975 o/p). Designed for students in the so-called Third World, this little book is straightforward, attractively so, and its illustrations, many of which are drawn from the Third World, are refreshingly novel to the Western reader.

Recently there has been a spate of books introducing Paul, his background, his theology, his letters. Perhaps the best of these is Joseph A. Fitzmyer's *Paul and His Theology: A Brief Sketch* (/Prentice-Hall 1989 $17.00 pb). Neal Flanagan's *Friend Paul: His Letters, Theology and Humanity* (Glazier 1991/1986 £7.50/$9.95) is very elementary, but generally competent. Most of these books do not treat all the Paulines, judging some of them to be deuterocanonical; Flanagan omits the Pastorals, and dates 1 Thessalonians before Galatians (still the majority view). The recent book by Martin Hengel, in collaboration with Roland Deines, *The Pre-Christian Paul* (SCM/TPI 1991 £10.95/$21.95), is of very great importance, not only for understanding Paul's background and the combination of Judaism and Hellenism from which he springs, but also for the implicit analysis of the theses of E. P. Sanders. The second edition of Leander E. Keck's *Paul and His Letters* (ProcC; 1988 /$9.95) has been superseded by Fitzmyer. Stanley B. Morrow's *Paul: His Letters and His Theology* (Paulist 1986 £9.95/$9.95) can be ignored, as can Marion L. Soards' *The Apostle Paul: An Introduction to His Writings and Teaching* (Paulist 1987 £7.50/$9.95). Harold Weiss's *Paul of Tarsus: His Gospel and Life* (/Andrews University Press 1986 pb np) is one of the better elementary introductions.

There are countless special studies relating to Romans, only very few of which can be mentioned here. There are stimulating and provocative essays in E. Käsemann's *New Testament Questions for Today* and *Perspectives on Paul*, both o/p. G. Bornkamm's *Paul* is still available (Hodder 1975 £7.99 / Harper 1971 $17.95). But the book that has precipitated much of the current debate on Paul and the law is doubtless that of E. P. Sanders, *Paul and Palestinian Judaism* (SCM 1981 £15.00 / Fortress 1977 $24.95 pb). To this must now be added his book *Paul, the Law, and the Jewish People* (SCM 1985 £12.50 pb / Fortress 1983 $12.95 pb). His smaller and more recent *Paul* (OUP 1991 £4.99/$5.95) adds little to his fundamental theses. Many books and essays have either taken Sanders on board, or in some measure reacted against him, and this work inevitably affects the commentaries on Paul as well. Major work needs to be done in this area. Well worth reading, if you can pick it up s/h, is W. D. Davies' *Paul and Rabbinic Judaism* (4th ed. 1980 o/p). His *Jewish and Pauline Studies* (1984, also o/p) is not so cohesive. Nevertheless, these books reflect a lifetime of study, and will repay the student or minister who is well enough equipped to handle them. Mention must be made of Seyoon Kim's *The Origin of Paul's Gospel* (regrettably o/p), who argues that the basic structure of Paul's thought is tied up with his conversion on the Damascus road. In some ways this is an impressive updating of the old work by J. Gresham Machen, *The Origin of Paul's Religion* (o/p), but in addition to the thesis, the book is studded with valuable discussions and exegeses. Harry Gamble, Jr.'s *The Textual History of the Letter to the Romans* (o/p) provides an able defense of the unity of the epistle. The best exegetical and theological discussion of Romans 9 is that of John Piper, *The Justification of God: An Exegetical and Theological Study of Romans 9:1-23*, which is being reprinted by Baker (forthcoming, 1993). For those interested in the history of the study of the Pauline epistles (or at least some of them), I should perhaps mention another work that has come out since the last edition of this survey, John Locke's *A Paraphrase and Notes on the Epistles of St. Paul to the Galatians, 1 and 2 Corinthians, Romans, Ephesians*, ed. by Arthur W. Wainwright (2 vols.; OUP 1987 £50.00 and £45.00 respectively / $98.00 and $89.00 respectively). Finally, of all the books that wrestle with Pauline theology, probably the best is Herman Ridderbos' *Paul: An Outline of His Theology* (o/p / Eerdmans 1975 np).

### 3.07 1 Corinthians

The best general commentary on this epistle is doubtless that of *Gordon D. Fee* (NIC; /Eerdmans 1987 $32.95). Despite one or two extraordinary lapses (e.g., his treatment of 1 Corinthians 4:33b–35 as an interpolation), the commentary is lucid, informed, and written with great verve. Scarcely less important is *C. K. Barrett* (BNTC/ HNTC 2d ed. Black 1971 £10.99 pb / Hendrickson 1987 [1968] $19.95). In both cases there is a wealth of useful material, and those with minimal Greek can follow the argument. *F. F. Bruce* on both the Corinthian epistles (NCB 1981/1980 £8.95/$10.95) is astonishingly good for the space allotted: the work is a marvel of condensed learning, and especially wise on certain contentious issues (e.g., the χαρίσματα), but the brevity of the discussion forces the reader to turn to longer works. *Roy A. Harrisville* (ACNT 1987 /$14.95) is useful, but cannot compete with Fee and Barrett. Charles H. Talbert's *Reading Corinthians: A New Commentary for Preachers* [=British subtitle; American subtitle is *A Literary and Theological Commentary on 1 and 2 Corinthians*] (SPCK/Crossroad 1987 £9.99 pb/$11.95) is often helpful in identifying literary patterns and flow, but is theologically rather thin, and rarely treats the text verse by verse. He thinks 2 Cor.10–13 was written before 2 Corinthians 1–9.

Perhaps the standard critical commentary on the Greek text of 1 Corinthians is that of *Hans Conzelmann* (Hermeneia; 1975 £20.00/$29.95). Its extensive bibliography and full citation of parallel texts, not to mention its frequently penetrating discussion, make it invaluable to students who can handle Greek. Moreover most of the cited texts provide full ET. But the substantial weakness of the work cannot be ignored (cf. the review in *Themelios* 1 [1976]: 56–57). The old ICC volume by *Archibald Robertson* and *Alfred Plummer* (2d ed. 1914 £17.50/$29.95) adduces many parallels without the benefit of translation, but this work is one of the better ones in the series. Other works largely on the Greek text include *J. Héring* (ET from 2d French ed. 1948; o/p), which maintains a partition theory but is full of useful and spritely comment. The little book by *R. St. John Parry* (CGT 2d ed. 1937 o/p) is helpful to the student trying to sharpen Greek skills, if it can be obtained s/h.

Other commentaries deserving honorable mention include *J. S. Ruef* (Pelican; 1977 o/p), which is competent and makes good use of space, but does not add much to Barrett and Bruce; and in the revised edition (TNTC; IVP 1986 £4.50 / Eerdmans 1988 $8.95), who provides useful remarks on some Greek words behind the ET. *James Moffatt* (Moffatt; 1938 o/p) is still worth scanning on the religious, social, and historical background in Hellenism. *C. T. Craig* (IB vol. 10, bound with 2 Corinthians and Ephesians; 1953 £21.50/np) adds some useful comments here and there, but the expense of the entire volume does not justify the purchase. *W. F. Orr* and *J. A. Walther* (AB; 1976 /$20.00) provide a very lengthy introduction that is very concerned with Paul's itinerary and its relation to Acts, frequently for the (laudable) purpose of rehabilitating Acts; but it contains too little information on Corinth, and the comments themselves vary from the very detailed to the very thin. Karl Barth's *The Resurrection of the Dead* (repr. of 1933 ed.; /Ayer 1977 $23.50) is still an outstanding work. Although this is primarily only an exposition of chapter 15, the first half of the book offers a résumé of the argument of the first fourteen chapters. There can be few better expositions of the grace of God and the frailty of humankind than this little book. It is certainly not a verse-by-verse commentary.

J. B. Lightfoot's *Notes on the Epistles of St. Paul* has often been reprinted, but is now o/p. Lightfoot is always worth consulting, although usually later commentaries have gleaned the best of his work. Available reprints include: *Hermann Olshausen* [on both Corinthian epistles] (/Kregel nd $16.95), which varies between the insightful and the eccentric; *Thomas C. Edwards* (/Kregel nd $18.95); and *Charles Hodge* (BoT 1974/1978 £11.50/$24.95), which is not as good as some have thought. Doubtless it was outstanding when there was less exegetical competition, and it is still worth perusing today— but not as a first choice, and only if allowance is made for a century of work, including considerable improvement in our grasp of Hellenistic Greek. Bernard O'Kelly has edited John Colet's [d.1519] *Commentary on First Corinthians: A New Edition of the Latin Text, with Translation, Annotations* (Brighamton, N.Y.: Medieval and Renaissance Texts and Studies, 1985; $24.00), which will doubtless prove of greater help to students of the Renaissance and of the history of exegesis than to students of 1 Corinthians.

*G. Deluz* (1963 o/p) is excellent from a practical point of view, read in conjunction with a commentary like that of Fee or Barrett. Deluz tends to summarize the best of points from *F. Godet* (2 vols. repr. as one; /Kregel 1982/1977 £19.95/$37.95). *F. W. Grosheide*, the old NIC work (1953 o/p) now replaced by Fee, is at best average: generally clear, not very deep, and with no outstanding merit. Both *Robert B. Hughes* (/Moody 1985 $6.95) and *John J. Kilgallen* (Paulist 1987 £5.95/$5.95), although from very different theological backgrounds, share this in common: their books are primarily for the general reader within their respective constituencies. *Kenneth L. Chafin* (CC; 1985 np) can be safely ignored. Alan Redpath's *The Royal Route to Heaven* (o/p) is completely unreliable on exegesis, but where his own thoughts coincide with the sense of the passage, they are remarkably practical. *Marcus Dods* (EB; o/p) is verbose but worth scanning. *Gordon H. Clark* (2d ed.; /Trinity Foundation 1989 $9.95) tends to treat the text in a historical vacuum, and sometimes reveals more about himself and his beliefs than his ostensible subject, but occasionally there are insightful remarks. *Margaret E. Thrall* (CBC; 1965 £9.95 pb/$11.95 pb) is one of the best of the brief commentaries, but the final essay, on "The Corinthian Letters Today," is rather misleading. *W. Baird* (KPG; 1980 /$4.95) and *J. Murphy-O'Connor* (NTM; 1980 £3.25 pb/$8.95) are both worth scanning. *John MacArthur, Jr.* (/Moody 1984 $16.95) provides more of an exposition than a commentary (see remarks on his work on Matthew). Despite excellent moments, there is too little grasp of the background, and such firm "anticharismatic" interpretation of chapters 12–14, that the exegesis goes a little awry.

There are numerous special studies on 1 Corinthians, or on the pair of Corinthian epistles, and a few of them deserve mention here. Jerome Murphy-O'Connor's *St. Paul's Corinth: Texts and Archaeology* (/Liturgical 1983 $12.95 pb) is invaluable for those who want more background information. J. C. Hurd, Jr.'s *The Origin of 1 Corinthians* (rev. ed. 1982; o/p) provides a detailed reconstruction of the situation at Corinth, but the theory is supported by considerable speculation and highly improbable partition theories. Hurd's work now enjoys less influence than it once did. A quiet little gem is Lewis B. Smedes' *Love within Limits: Realizing Selfless Love in a Selfish World* [=orig. subtitle; recently changed to *A Realist's View of 1 Corinthians*] (/Eerdmans 1978 $5.95 pb), which uses 1 Corinthians 13 as the basis for some thoughtful and sometimes stirring reflections. *Ralph P. Martin* has written the Word Biblical Themes volume on 1–2 Corinthians (/Word 1989 np); the same author has published *The Spirit and the Congregation: Studies in 1 Corinthians 12–15* (1984 o/p). The latter is written in an easy style that belies the work that has gone into it, but I found it more reliable on chapter 15 than on chapters 12–14. D. A. Carson's *Showing the Spirit: A Theological Exposition of 1 Corinthians 12–14* (Paternoster/Baker 1987 np/$12.95) attempts a fairly detailed exegesis of the three chapters specified in the title, and a discussion of their relation to relevant passages in Acts and to modern developments. It includes a full bibliography and detailed notes, although the text itself can be followed by the student without Greek. Forthcoming is D. A. Carson's *The Cross and Christian Ministry: Studies in 1 Corinthians* (/Baker, 1993), a series of expository studies on parts of 1 Corinthians, originally prepared for IFES. Wayne Grudem's *The Gift of Prophecy in 1 Corinthians* (/UPA 1982) is now o/p, but one can still find his argument, if not the focus on 1 Corinthians, in his more recent and general *The Gift of Prophecy in the New Testament and Today* (Kingsway/Crossway 1988 £7.95/$12.95).

## 3.08 2 Corinthians

I shall not mention again those commentaries that serve both of the epistles to the Corinthians (discussed above). After years of neglect, 2 Corinthians has now attracted some—but only some—of the attention it deserves. It is the most passionate and in some ways the most difficult of Paul's letters.

*C. K. Barrett* (BNTC/HNTC; 1973 £10.99 / 1974 $19.95 [strangely, Hendrickson also has a 1987 repr. of the 1973 ed., $19.95]) is quite outstanding. One may disagree with Barrett's breakdown of opponents in chapters 10–13, and with other minor points, but this commentary is one of the "standard" works. Another is the recent work by *Victor Paul Furnish* (AB; 1984 /$24.00). Much longer than Barrett, this one leaves few stones unturned, and on many points offers sane and thoughtful exegesis. Of similar length is the recent work by *Ralph P. Martin* (WBC; 1985 /$25.99). As usual, Martin displays a mastery of most of the secondary literature, and as usual writes with clarity; but I found the work a little disappointing, too speculative at many junctures, and occasionally wrong-headed. The ET of the CNT volume by *Jean Héring* (1965 o/p) is sprightly and well written but now superseded by Barrett and Furnish.

*Philip Hughes* (NIC; 1982 /$24.95) provides thoughtful and usually reliable comments, but lacks verve and power. *R. V. G. Tasker* (TNTC; o/p) is well written and briefly helpful, but adds nothing to Hughes. In any case it has been superseded by the new TNTC volume, by *Colin Kruse* (1987 £3.95/$6.95)—an excellent addition to the series. *A. Plummer* (ICC; 1915 £17.50/$29.95) tends to be pedestrian, but is worth picking up s/h. *F. V. Filson* (IB vol. 10; see above on 1 Corinthians) sometimes adds fresh insight, but not everyone will want to pay the price for the whole volume. *R. H. Strachan* (Moffatt; 1935 o/p) obviously had a bad year in 1935. *James Denney* (EB; nd o/p) is still very fresh on many issues, but it would seem better if it had not been overrated by some senior evangelicals. *J. H. Bernard* (EGNT; 5-vol. set ed. W. Robertson Nicoll; /Eerdmans 1952 $89.95 the set) is dated but sometimes useful. *M. J. Harris* (EBC vol. 10; see on Romans) is quite excellent within the strictures of space allotted to it—clearly the best of the four commentaries bound up in this volume. Harris is currently working on the NIGTC volume on 2 Corinthians *Frederick W. Danker* (ACNT; 1989 /$14.95) is worth scanning, but cannot compete with Barrett and Furnish; the same is true of *E. Best* (Interpretation; John Knox 1987 £12.95/$16.95). *Richard P. C. Hanson* (TBC; 1961 o/p) is slender but worth skimming; much the same can be said for *G. R. Beasley-Murray* (Broadman; o/p). Barely worth scanning, as far as the preacher is concerned, is the ET of *Rudolf Bultmann* (/Augsburg 1985 o/p; the German original was 1976, published from class notes of lectures delivered between 1940 and 1952).

In the BST series, *Paul Barnett*'s work is well done (1988 £5.25/$11.95). H. D. Betz's *2 Corinthians 8 and 9* (Hermeneia; 1986/1985 £21.50/$29.95) is typical Betz: many parallels, only some of which are exegetically helpful, and too little theological reflection. Despite its title and series, the work by Jerome Murphy-O'Connor, *The Theology of the Second Letter to the Corinthians* (NTT; 1991 £22.50 hb or £7.95pb / $29.95 hb or $10.95 pb), is less a theological analysis of 2 Corinthians than a flowing survey, with some probing into the social background. D. A. Carson's *From Triumphalism to Maturity: An Exposition of 2 Corinthians 10–13* (IVP/Baker 1986 £4.95 pb/$7.95 pb) is, as the subtitle suggests, an exposition of the last four chapters of 2 Corinthians, the most emotionally explosive writings from Paul's pen.

The record of greater or lesser disappointments from the past includes *Francis T. Fallon* (NTM; 1980 £3.25/$8.95); Alan Redpath's *Blessings out of Buffetings: Studies in Second Corinthians* (/Revell 1965 $12.95)—see the comments on his volume on 1 Corinthians; and the following three reprints: *Roy L. Laurin* (/Kregel 1985 $10.95); *H. C. G. Moule* (/CLC 1976 $4.95); *Charles R. Erdman* (orig. 1929, often reprinted, just o/p again).

## 3.09 Galatians

There are two recent commentaries on the Greek text, each in its own way outstanding. *Hans Dieter Betz* (Hermeneia; 1980/1979 £22.00/$29.95) provides voluminous parallels from the Greco-Roman world, including almost endless comment on the kinds and style of argument Paul deploys. His use of Jewish background is disappointingly thin, and the salvation-historical structure of parts of Paul's argument sometimes overlooked. I do not think he has got to the bottom of Paul's understanding of the relationships between law and grace. F. F. Bruce (NIGTC; 1982 £19.50 hb or £12.50 pb / np) evenhandedly weighs virtually all of the relevant literature, and presents the flow of the argument with a deft touch and readable prose. Occasionally the reader will want more theological punch, such as on the law/grace, old covenant/new covenant fronts, and in more detailed dialogue with E. P. Sanders and his followers. Criticisms aside, these two commentaries are very important, if the student or preacher can work with the Greek text. Not surprisingly, homiletical hints are few and far between.

Based on the Greek text, but more accessible to the reader without much skill in Greek, are the recent commentaries by *Richard N. Longenecker* (WBC; 1990 /$24.99) and *Ronald Y. K. Fung* (NIC; 1988 $22.95). The latter is workmanlike and a substantial improvement over its predecessor in the series; the former is especially strong on the Jewish roots of the debate, but perhaps weaker on Spirit-passages.

*John Bligh* (St. Paul Pub./ 1969 £16.00/$60.00) has produced a 500-pp. commentary that represents the best of modern Roman Catholic scholarship in England, although he still includes oddly loaded comments on such issues as the role of Peter. The structuralism is plentiful, perhaps forced at times. Although there is much to admire, I am not convinced that Paul always speaks for himself. The commentary by *Donald Guthrie* (NCB; 1982/1981 £6.95; $10.95), as we have come to expect from this author, is always clear, ordered, and on the whole valuable, even if sometimes not very incisive. The CBC commentary by *William Neil* (1967/1966 £7.50 pb/$9.50 pb) is stimulating, but too brief to demand much attention. The contribution by *Charles Cousar* (Interpretation; John Knox 1986/1982 £12.95/$15.95) is even less full, but is one of the better contributions to this series. The ET of the work by *Ragnar Bring* (1961 o/p) is oriented in the direction of Lutheran dogmatics.

*E. de W. Burton* (ICC; 1921 £19.95/$29.95) remains a monument of thoroughness and concern over detail. The additional notes are often useful, as well as the comments, but the latter have largely been superseded by Betz and Bruce. Concise and occasionally useful to the preacher are the practical commentaries by *K. Grayston* (1957 o/p) and *G. S. Duncan* (Moffatt; 1934 o/p). The latter can often be picked up s/h. *H. N. Ridderbos* (NL/NIC 1953 o/p) has now been superseded by its replacement volume by Ronald Y. K. Fung. *William Hendriksen* (NTC; Gal. in one volume: BoT 1969 £5.50; Galatians and Ephesians bound together: BoT 1981 £12.95 /Baker 1979 $24.95) is warm-hearted, but too frequently misses the historical and theological nuances of the text. *R. Alan Cole* (TNTC; 1983/1989 £4.25/ $6.95) is sometimes helpful in bringing out the meaning of Greek terms simply and concisely. *James Montgomery Boice* (EBC vol. 10; see on Romans) is helpful enough for the preacher, but adds nothing to, say, Guthrie.

*J. B. Lightfoot* (repr. as 3-vol. set on Galatians, Philippians, Colossians, & Philemon; /Hendrickson 1981 $49.95) has been mined so thoroughly by others that he hardly ever adds anything to more modern treatments. *Martin Luther*'s work is available in at least two English-language editions, the former somewhat abridged (Clarke 1953 £8.95 / Kregel repr. 1987 $12.95; and vols. 26–27 of the Concordia set of Luther's works, ed. J. Pelikan, 1962–63, at $18.95 and $19.95 respectively). He writes with power and passion, but his work is simply too verbose for most twentieth-century readers, who in any case need to make allowance for Luther's concern with the pope in places where Paul is concerned with Moses. J. Skilton has edited Machen's *Notes on Galatians* (unfortunately o/p). This is not strictly a commentary, nor does it cover the entire epistle, and in any case it is very dated. But the student who works through it carefully will learn what exegesis is all about, how to do it, and even how to apply it to a contemporary setting (although some of the historical allusions reflect the struggles of a past generation). Specialists may appreciate the ET of Desiderius Erasmus' *Paraphrases on Romans and Galatians*, ed. Robert D. Sider, tr. John B. Payne et al. (vol. 42 of the *Collected Works*; /University of Toronto 1984 $50.00). They will also appreciate the availability of the classic commentary by *William A. Perkins* (/Pilgrim 1989 [1617] np), one of the strategic transitional figures in the move from the continental to the English Reformation.

A number of smaller, lighter commentaries have appeared, including one by *Edgar Krentz* on Galatians; *John Koenig* on Philippians and Philemon; *Donald H. Juel* on 1 Thessalonians—all bound together (ACNT; 1985 /$13.95), and another by *Leroy E. Lawson* (/Standard 1987 $12.95 pb). The latter is not up to snuff, and the former is too brief to compete with more substantial work. *John MacArthur, Jr.* (/Moody 1987 $12.95) often makes some very good pastoral points that are helpful to the preacher, but he should not be used on his own (see comments on his Matthew]. The same could be said for the devotional classic by Lehman Strauss, *Galatians and Ephesians* (/Loizeaux 1957 $10.95).

Many popular expositions have been written on Galatians, but only a few of them deserve skimming, let alone thoughtful reading. One of the best is John Stott's *Only One Way: The Message of Galatians* (BST; 1984 £5.25 / 1988 $11.95). William Barclay's little study *Flesh and Spirit* (St. Andrew Press 1978 £2.50/) is helpful, and the price is right. *W. A. Criswell* (1980) is now o/p, but in this case the loss is not great. The Baker repr. of *Charles Erdman* is now itself o/p. The contribution of *Carolyn Osiek* (NTM; 1981 £2.45/$12.95 hb or $6.95 pb) is one of the thinnest in the series.

The work by Gerhard Ebeling, *The Truth of the Gospel* (Fortress 1985 £19.25 / o/p), is a cross between a running exposition and an essay in systematic theology. Based on the Greek text (which is then both transliterated and translated), the book is fresh and stimulating, but like so many other tomes written from a Lutheran and existential perspective, it is frequently right in what it affirms and wrong in what it denies—especially on crucial topics such as faith, truth, law, and works of the law. The study by John Barclay, *Obeying the Truth: A Study of Paul's Ethics in Galatians* (T & T Clark 1988 £18.95/$34.95), is very strong when it focuses on the exegesis of the last two chapters, and worth the most careful reading for that reason. But I am not sure that Barclay, who has bought into rather more of E. P. Sanders than seems justifiable, has rightly sorted out how Paul thinks of the relationship between law and grace. Somewhat irritating is Barclay's tendency on occasion to be so kind to Paul's opponents that he makes Paul sound like a twit.

## 3.10 Ephesians

The best English-language commentary on Ephesians is now that of *Andrew T. Lincoln* (WBC; 1990 /$24.99). On grounds that strike me as entirely unconvincing, Lincoln argues that Paul himself did not

write Ephesians, and occasionally this stance affects his exegesis (e.g.,
on 4:7ff.). On the whole, however, it does not, and the commentary
on many passages is superb, both at the level of dealing faithfully with
the text, and at the level of theological reflection. Lincoln's grasp of
the eschatology of the epistle is profound. Not as thorough, but nevertheless an important work, is the ET of *Rudolf Schnackenburg* (T
& T Clark 1991 24.95/$49.95).

The longest commentary is that of *Markus Barth* (AB; 2 vols. 1975
o/p). It is painstakingly detailed, but even so the theology sometimes
dictates to the exegesis. More advanced students can scarcely afford
to be without it. But Barth's treatment of certain themes crucial to
the epistle sounds more like his father than like Paul. In some ways,
a more useful commentary is that of *C. L. Mitton* (NCB 1982/1981
£6.95/$12.95). In general this is a good and accessible work, even if
Mitton continues to support his earlier defense of non-Pauline authorship. He apparently had no opportunity to interact with A. Van Roon's
substantial defense of the traditional position, in *The Authenticity of
Ephesians* (SuppNovT 39; Brill 1974 o/p). (Intriguingly, Lincoln
reviewed van Roon at one point, and offered additional reasons to
support van Roon's position! Thus his commentary marks a change
from his earlier published stance.) The metamorphosis from GNC
(1984) to NIBC has been successfully accomplished for *Arthur G.
Patzia*'s work on Ephesians, Colossians, and Philippians (1991 /$9.95
pb); the result is a competent but unexciting middle-level commentary, easily accessible. *Francis Beare* (IB vol. 10) is scarcely worth scanning. *Ernest Scott* (Moffatt; 1939 o/p) is erratic and uneven. *Francis
Foulkes* (TNTC; 1989 £4.25/$7.95) offers good value for its size.
(Incidentally, one must constantly examine what a new "edition"
means. During the early 1980s, many of the TNTC and NCB volumes came out in new pb editions, therefore boasting a new date,
even though all that had changed was the cover: the text was that of
work done ten or twenty or more years earlier. The latest TNTC editions, however, are either updated work by the same author, or commentaries by new authors replacing the earlier contributors.) The
ACNT contribution to Ephesians and Colossians, by *Walter F. Taylor, Jr.* and *John H. P. Reumann* respectively (1985 /$13.95), is ade-
quate but undistinguished.

*H. K. Moulton* (with Colossians; Epworth/ 1962 o/p) has a good
eye for practical lessons, but should not be used on its own. *E. K.
Simpson*, in an earlier edition of NL/NIC (1957/1958 o/p), pro-

vides some helpful comments on individual words, but on the whole the work is an erudite disappointment. His vocabulary is impressive, but not much else. The replacement by *F. F. Bruce* (on Ephesians, Colossians, and Philippians; 1984 /$22.95) marked a notable advance; his work is well worth reading, even though Lincoln has on most points now eclipsed him. One should also not overlook Bruce's more popular exposition (Pickering and Inglis 1978 £2.95 / o/p). Neither *J. A. Allan* (TBC; 1959 o/p) nor *G. H. P. Thompson* (CBC, with Colossians and Philemon; 1967 £10.95/) is very significant. *A. Skevington Wood* (EBC vol.11; 1978 /$26.95) is not worth much time.

Brief commentaries on the so-called prison epistles (Ephesians, Philippians, Colossians, and Philemon) bound in one volume have been written by *J. Leslie Houlden* (Pelican; 1977 o/p) and *George B. Caird* (NClar; 1976 £4.95 pb/$19.95 pb [the latter figure is larcenous]). They pack a great deal into small scope, especially the latter. By contrast, the work on Ephesians, Philippians, and Colossians by *George Johnston* (CB; 1967 o/p) is disappointingly thin just where one needs the most guidance. The book by *John F. MacArthur, Jr.* (/Moody 1986 $14.95) shares the same strengths and weaknesses as his treatment of Matthew.

The old-fashioned standby on the Greek text is *J. Armitage Robinson*, now regrettably o/p. It can still be very useful, though its best points have been culled by Bruce and Lincoln. *B. F. Westcott* (o/p) is almost as good, and his additional notes repay rapid perusal. *S. D. Salmond* (EGNT; the entire set, /Eerdmans 1952 $89.95) completes this older classical trio. *Charles Hodge* (BoT repr. 1991 £7.95/$21.95) is even older, but solid, often theologically very suggestive. One should certainly not overlook John Calvin's *Sermons on Ephesians* (BoT repr. 1974/1979 £13.95/$28.95), which can still be marvelously suggestive to preachers. The classic work by *George Stoeckhardt* has now been translated (/Concordia 1987 $17.95).

Of the more popular treatments, the studies by *H. C. G. Moule* (/Kregel 1977 [1937] $7.95) still offer good value for money. The eight volumes of sermons by *D. Martyn Lloyd-Jones* (BoT 1976-1985, @ various prices from £6.95 to £12.95—some of them hb only, some available in pb / Baker 1983 $119.95 the set) is eminently worth reading, but only if you read very quickly. Worth reading, too, is John R. W. Stott's *God's New Society* (BST; 1984/1988 £6.25/$11.95). *Lionel Swain* (NTM; 1981 £3.25/$10.95 hb or $5.95 pb) is not worth the time. The expositions by *James M. Boice* (/Zondervan

1988 $12.95 pb) and *R. Kent Hughes* (/Crossway 1990 $13.95) are
models of their kind, and well worth reading: they demonstrate the
best of expository ministry, and become models for preachers. *Homer
Kent, Jr.* (/Moody 1971 $5.95) is not as good. The little book by
Donald Guthrie, *Exploring God's Word: Bible Guide to Ephesians,
Philippians and Colossians* (Hodder & Stoughton 1984 o/p / Eerdmans 1985 $6.95), is designed to encourage inductive Bible study
among laypeople.

For those who read French, the commentary by *Charles Masson*
(CNT; o/p) is outstanding, although well culled by Lincoln. Spe-
cialists may also want to read Edgar J. Goodspeed's *The Meaning of
Ephesians* (/University of Chicago Press 1933 o/p).

## 3.11 Philippians

By far the best commentary on the Greek text of Philippians is the
majesterial work by *Peter T. O'Brien* (NIGTC; 1991 /$39.95).
O'Brien has read and thought through everything of importance, with
the result that he gives reasons for his exegetical decisions. At the same
time, this commentary is theologically rich, even if its prose is sometimes pedestrian. The treatment of the so-called Christ hymn (2:5–11)
is superb. More accessible to students and pastors who have not kept
their Greek up is *Gerald Hawthorne* (WBC; 1983 np). Hawthorne's
strength is the culling of scholarship up to his time. But his work pre-
sents some highly implausible comments (e.g., on 1:27–30, where his
reading of the Greek is just about impossible, and on the "hymn,"
where he opts for the Byz reading to solve the parallelism). *Moisés
Silva* (BECNT; 1992 /$19.95) is excellent for its relative brevity, and
is especially strong in tracing the flow of the argument, but it is rather
brief, interacts with little of the literature, and is in any case outstripped
by O'Brien. Farther down the list of recent commentaries is *Fred B.
Craddock* (Interpretation; 1986/1984 £12.95/$13.95).

*J. B. Lightfoot* continues to be reprinted (see on Galatians), and his
additional essays are still valuable. *M. R. Vincent* (ICC, including Philemon; 1897 £14.95/$24.95) adds virtually nothing to the more recent
commentaries. *F. W. Beare* has just come back into print (NCB; 1988
[1959] £8.99 pb/), but the work is too brief, and defends partition
theories that sometimes affect the exegesis. His comments are sometimes very astute (e.g., on righteousness). *R. P. Martin* has written
two commentaries on this epistle, one of them now extensively revised.

The earlier one, in the TNTC series, was originally published in 1960, and was reprinted in a pb edition in 1983. Given its scope, it is excellent, and still worth obtaining s/h (it is o/p). In the most recent edition of this TNTC commentary, however (1987/1988 £4.25/$6.95), Martin has revised his work to bring it into line with his NCB commentary on Philippians (1981/1980 £5.95/$10.95). This is packed with useful interaction with the secondary literature, but by this point Martin was influenced by Käsemann's "odyssey of Christ" approach to the Philippians hymn and related material. I find this interpretation exegetically weak. The matter is well discussed by O'Brien. *J. H. Michael* (Moffatt; o/p) contains many useful hints for the preacher, if the commentary is read in conjunction with a more rigorous work. *F. F. Bruce*, after the usual metamorphosis from GNC, has contributed the NIBC volume on Philippians (1989 /$9.95). It is brief and to the point. A solid, verbose, and unexciting treatment can be found in *W. Hendriksen* (bound with Colossians and Philemon; BoT 1988 $12.95 / Baker 1979 $22.95).

The two commentaries on the prison epistles I mentioned in the Ephesians section, by *J. L. Houlden* and *George B. Caird*, are worth scanning. A number of older or shorter commentaries are generally unremarkable. *F. Synge* (TBC; 1951 o/p) is too brief to give much help (except for a good comment on Christ as "Adam in reverse" in 2:1–11). The substantial work by *Jean-François Collange* is still available in English (Epworth/TPI 1979 £8.50/$12.95), and even in translation is forceful and provocative, but his judgments can be questioned too often to make this a first choice. *K. Grayston* (with 1–2 Thessalonians; CBC; 1984 /$16.95 pb), in spite of its brevity, is sometimes worth scanning. *H. A. A. Kennedy* (EGNT; 5 vols.; Eerdmans 1952 $89.95 the set) and *Jacobus J. Müller* (NIC; 1985 [1955] /$22.95) are severely dated, and were never that outstanding in the first place. The same must be said for *Alfred Plummer* (o/p). *Homer A. Kent* (EBC; for details see on Ephesians) is brief and was dated when it was written; it sometimes has useful remarks on individual words. H. C. G. Moule continues to be reprinted (/Kregel 1977 /$6.95), largely because of the warm, devotional tone that embraces his exegesis.

Specialists will be sorry to discover that R. P. Martin's *Carmen Christi* (2d ed. 1983) is again o/p. For bibliographical thoroughness up to its time of publication, it is impossible to beat.

Countless popular studies on Philippians have been prepared, many with the word "joy" in the title somewhere. The best of them include:

A. T. Robertson's *Paul's Joy in Christ*, recently (1979) repr. by Baker, but again o/p; J. Alec Motyer's *The Message of Philippians: Jesus our Joy* (BST; 1984/1988 £5.95/$11.95); James M. Boice's *Philippians: An Expositional Commentary* (/Zondervan 1982 $11.95); John Gwyn-Thomas' *Rejoice . . . Always!* (BoT 1990 np), a study in Philippians 4; Earl Palmer's *Integrity in a World of Pretense: Insights from the Book of Philippians* (/IVP 1991 $14.95); and Gerald F. Hawthorne, who in addition to his WBC commentary has produced the Word Biblical Themes volume (1987 /$8.95).

### 3.12 Colossians/Philemon

Several major commentaries on Colossians press for attention. Probably the best is that of *Peter T. O'Brien* (WBC; 1987/1982 £7.95 pb/np). Based on an exact exegesis of the Greek text, it is nevertheless presented with sufficient clarity to satisfy most readers who do not know the language. It is a mine of useful bibliography and helpful interaction with secondary literature, and wends its way through voluminous material without losing its theological moorings. Equally scholarly is the work of *E. Lohse* (Hermeneia; 1971 £17.50/$24.95). The reader should not be put off by its rejection of Paul's authorship, for it too contains a wealth of clear and useful comment. A little more Greek is required of the reader, although parallels are usually provided both in the original and in translation. The 1987 German commentary by *Petr Pokorny* has been translated into English (/Hendrickson 1991 $19.95), but it adds little to the other two. Despite the relative dates, Pokorny does not seem to know of O'Brien. Pokorny comments only on Colossians; the other two include Philemon. Another recent commentary is the replacement TNTC volume by *N. T. Wright* (1987/1988 £4.25/$6.95). In some ways this is superb, and written with verve and style. I am not entirely persuaded by Wright's reconstruction of the situation Paul is confronting. In a class by itself is the inaugural EGGNT volume by *Murray J. Harris* (with Philem.; 1991 /$21.95). This is not quite a commentary, yet it is more than a commentary. Harris intends to help students and pastors read through the Greek text intelligently, making appropriate exegetical decisions at every point. He has gleaned the best of the grammars and commentaries with this purpose in mind, and thus saves the student a lot of time. Nevertheless his work does not replace the best commentaries, which offer far more theological reflection based on the text (but without always showing how it is tied to the text). Those who want short-cuts will give Harris a miss; those who want to improve their own exegetical skills on the way toward biblical theology will find him a very helpful guide. His book presupposes that the reader has had at least a couple of years of Greek.

The EKK volume on Colossians by *Eduard Schweizer* has been translated into English, but is no longer available (/Augsburg 1982 o/p). His work combines full knowledge of the relevant literature with some down-to-earth exegesis. The EKK volume on Philemon is separate, and there is no ET, but the German original by *Peter Stuhlmacher* is generally excellent (1975). I have often encouraged exegesis students to work through *C. F. D. Moule* (CGT 1957 £27.50 hb or £12.50 pb / $39.50 hb or $15.95 pb), a slim and outrageously priced book that forces the student to work with the Greek text. It has now been superseded by Harris and O'Brien. *F. F. Bruce* is useful as usual in his NIC volume on Ephesians [replacing Simpson], Colossians, and Philemon (1984 /$22.95). At about the same level is *R. P. Martin* (NCB; 1982/1981 £5.95/$10.95), in some ways a better work than his corresponding volume on Philippians. Less detailed and technical, and with some direct aids for the preacher, is his work *Colossians: The Church's Lord and the Christian's Liberty* (/Attic 1972 $12.50).

The reprint of *J. B. Lightfoot*, already mentioned (see on Galatians), makes available his usual thorough but now dated treatment of the Greek text, to which the ICC by *T. K. Abbott* (1897 £17.50/$29.95) adds surprisingly little. *G. Johnston* (1967 o/p) is disappointing, as is *E. F. Scott* (see on Ephesians). *F. W. Beare* (IB, in vol. 11; 1955 £21.50 for vol. 11 / $324.95 the set) still repays study. *H. K. Moulton*'s helpful little work was noticed in the Ephesians section. In addition to *William Barclay*'s DSB on Philippians, Colossians, and the Thessalonians epistles (1975 £4.50 / $14.95), one of the best in the DSB series, there is his useful book entitled *The All-Sufficient Christ* (St. Andrew 1978 £2.50 / o/p). *Herbert Carson* wrote the old TNTC volume (1960 o/p), but it was one of the weaker entries in the series, and has now been eclipsed by its successor (by N. T. Wright).

Specialists will be interested in the collection of essays on Colossians edited by Fred O. Francis and Wayne A. Meeks, *Conflict at Colossae* (/SP 1973 o/p). The recent study by Norman R. Petersen, *Rediscovering Paul: Philemon and the Sociology of Paul's Narrative World* (Fortress 1985 £23.00/$28.95) is a mixed bag. Its vocabulary is drawn from the world of sociology, which is sometimes deployed in too heavy-handed a fashion. On many points Petersen is creative and suggestive, but he does not appear to know enough about first-century social history (as opposed to sociology) to warrant his conclusions.

Gordon H. Clark (1979 o/p) oscillates between the insightful and the ill-informed. William Hendriksen (NTC 1979) has already been mentioned under Philippians. The ET of the exposition by *Jean Daillé* [b. 1594 in France] produced by Klock and Klock (1983) is now o/p; the commentary by *John Eadie* is back in print (/Kregel nd $14.95). The expository commentary by *Charles Erdman*, one-time professor of practical theology at Princeton Seminary, is again o/p. *H. C. G. Moule* is as useful here as anywhere, as a supplement to a more substantial commentary (/Kregel repr. 1977 $6.95). *Patrick V. Rogers* (NTM; 1981 £3.25/$10.95 hb or $5.95 pb) adds little. The BST contribution by *R. C. Lucas, Fullness and Freedom* (1984/1988 £5.25/$11.95), is worth scanning; there is then little need to read Thomas Trevethan's *Our Joyful Confidence: The Lordship of Christ in Colossians* (1981 o/p). Some practical advice is found in *S. Cox* and *A. H. Drysdale* on Philemon (recently repr. by /Klock and Klock 1982 [1897], but again o/p)—not so much a commentary as a series of lectures on ministry, and some notes. The EBC contribution on Colossians is by Curtis Vaughan (see Ephesians for details). It is clear and straightforward, but adds little to the major volumes. *Arthur A. Rupprecht* has contributed the Philemon comments in the same volume. One of the better expositions is that of *R. Kent Hughes* (/Crossway 1989 $12.95).

### 3.13 Thessalonians

The best all-round commentary on the Greek text of these epistles is now that of *Charles A. Wanamaker* (NIGTC; 1990 /$29.95). Wanamaker is thorough, and usually sensitive to both literary and theological flow. For students and pastors who can handle Greek, this commentary falls into the "must" column. A little more accessible is the WBC volume by *F. F. Bruce* (1986/1982 £7.95/np). Characterized by Bruce's thoroughness and care for detail, the work is especially valuable in its introductory remarks, its careful delineation of the background, and its useful excursus on "The Antichrist." A standard is the BNTC/HNTC volume by *Ernest Best* (Black 1972 £9.99 / Hendrickson repr. 1987 $19.95), which is thorough and moderately conservative in most of its conclusions. No less competent is the work by *I. Howard Marshall* (NCB; 1983 /$12.95), which tends to build on the work by Best and carry the discussion through the literature published since Best's commentary appeared. It is therefore wise to read Marshall in conjunction with Best. Marshall replaces the earlier NCB volume by *Arthur L. Moore*, which was adequate and helpful within its space limitations but far too brief to be a first choice.

*Leon Morris* has contributed two commentaries on these epistles, and has revised both of them. His contribution to the NIC series (1991 /$27.95) tends virtually to eclipse his entry in the TNTC series (1985/1984 £4.25/$6.95). He has also now added the Word Biblical Themes volume to his treatment of these epistles (1989 np). *Robert L. Thomas* (EBC; for details see on Ephesians) is determinedly exegetical, but somehow manages to detect pretribulational dispensationalism where many of his readers will not find it. Something similar could be said for *D. Edmond Hiebert* (/Moody 1971 o/p), although this one is written with more warmth. *Earl Palmer* has provided a rather weak contribution to the GNC series (1985 £2.50 / o/p); I have not seen any transmutation into NIBC. *R. A. Ward* (1974 o/p) is a fine supplemental commentary for pastors, but it should be used in conjunction with a more detailed work. *Ernest W. Saunders* (KPG on Thessalonians, Philippians, and Philemon; 1981 /$4.95) is one of the better entries in the series, although clearly hampered by brevity. *D. E. H. Whiteley* (NClar; 1969 o/p) is a small but useful supplement. *William Neil* (Moffatt; o/p) is worth scanning, but is showing signs of age. Now bound with his work on the Pastoral epistles, *W. Hendriksen* (NTC; BoT 1983 £13.95 / Baker 1979 $24.95) is worth skimming but should be used in conjunction with fuller works. The commentary by *Kenneth Grayston* was mentioned under Philippians *Gary W. Demarest* has produced the CC entry on Thessalonians and the Pastorals (/Work 1984 $14.95), and it is a fairly strong entry in a weak series.

Among the older works, *James Denney* (EB; o/p) will make a good s/h supplement, though insufficient on its own. *James Moffatt* (EGNT; the 5-vol. set from /Eerdmans 1952 $89.95) can still be useful. *G. Milligan* in the older Macmillan series on the Greek text (i.e., comparable to Swete on Mark or Creed on Luke) has been reprinted (/Kregel nd $12.95), and is worth reading, even though in some respects it is terribly dated. *E. J. Bicknell* (WC; o/p) is of indifferent value; *J. E. Frame* (ICC; 1912 £17.50/$29.95) is not much better. *C. F. Hogg* and *W. E. Vine* produced a very simple commentary rather like Tenney on John, but with occasionally useful comments on individual words—but the reprint is itself o/p. The same is true of the Baker repr. of the exposition of *Charles Erdman.*

Specialists will want to read Charles H. Giblin's *The Threat to Faith* (1967 o/p), a detailed examination of 2 Thessalonians 2 and its relation to apocalyptic. Two recent "commentaries" that are not really commentaries will also draw their interest. Abraham Malherbe's *Paul and the Thessalonians: The Philosophic Tradition of Pastoral Care* (Fortress 1987 £9.25/$10.95) draws many interesting Greco-Roman parallels to Paul's approach to pastoral care in the Thessalonian letters. But Malherbe does not adequately work out the fundamental differences that arise from Paul's eschatological vision. Perhaps his forthcoming commentary will be better integrated. Robert Jewett's *The Thessalonian Correspondence: Pauline Rhetoric and Millenarian Piety* (Fortress 1986 £16.95/$24.95) develops sociological categories to explain Pauline rhetoric. By focusing so narrowly, both Malherbe and Jewett have shed a little fresh insight; by the same token, their studies seem rather reductionistic.

Again it may be worth mentioning the best foreign-language commentary on the Thessalonians epistles—almost certainly that of *Béda Rigaux* (EtBib; 1956).

### 3.14 Pastorals

These epistles are still not very well served by commentaries in English. The NIGTC commentary by *George W. Knight III* is forthcoming, but I have not seen it so I cannot comment. The AB volume on Titus alone, by *J. D. Quinn* (1990 /$28.00), is full of really excellent exegesis, even though he thinks that the Pastoral epistles "as we have them" probably stem from A.D. 80–85. The standard work most cited by scholars is *H. Conzelmann* and *M. Dibelius*, available in English in the Hermeneia series (1972 £19.00/$22.95). But the work has always been somewhat overrated, and it is probably too full and doubtless far too committed to an unbelievable reconstruction of early church history to be very useful to most pastors. *J. N. D. Kelly* (BNTC/HNTC; 1963 £7.99/ o/p) provides a useful all-round commentary, including some brief comments about the more naive assumptions that sometimes underlie computer criticism. One of the better commentaries is that by *Gordon D. Fee*, apparently available both in its GNC form (1984 /$9.95) and in its NIBC metamorphosis (1988 /$7.95). Despite a number of points where I find his exegesis unsatisfying, Fee has worked hard at building a more or less believable "life setting" that ties the contents of these three epistles together. *J. L. Houlden*'s earlier Pelican commentary (1976 o/p) has now been revised and placed in another series (TPINT; 1989 £12.50 hb or £6.50 pb / $14.95) and is worth perusing. *C. K. Barrett* (NClar; 1963 o/p) packs much material into little space. *Reginald H. Fuller* (ProcC with other authors on J. Paul Sampley on Ephesians, along with other authors on Colossians and 2 Thessalonians; 1978 £4.50 / o/p) is praised by some, but he is so tied to a late date and situation that all his exegesis is affected. *Donald Guthrie*, now in the revised edition (TNTC; 1990/1991 £4.50/$7.95), has become something of a classic not least because of its introduction and defense of Pauline authorship, but preachers will wish he had been given more space to erect an exegetical foundation and to locate the epistles in some focused situation. *Walter Lock* (ICC; 1928 £14.95/$24.95) is now hopelessly dated, but contains a number of perennially relevant observations. *Luke Timothy Johnson* (KPG; 1987 /$7.95) is one of the better ones in the series. *Thomas C. Oden* (Interpretation; /Westminster & John Knox 1989 $16.95) is a remarkable work. It is up-to-date, well written, and defends Pauline authorship. But it is not a traditional commentary: it organizes the pericopae topically, with the preacher in mind. This makes it harder to follow the flow of the text, but has some advantages for the preacher who is trying to group together some of the material Paul treats.

A. T. Hanson has followed his brief commentary (CBC; 1966 £7.95/$8.50) with a larger one (NCB; 1982 £8.95 pb/) and with some longer discussions in *Studies in the Pastoral Epistles* (1968 o/p). This concentrates on difficult passages, and the author often has some fresh suggestions to make, but the best of these have now been culled by the more recent commentaries. Not a commentary, but no less useful, is the brief study by George W. Knight III, *The Faithful Sayings in the Pastoral Epistles* (o/p). *E. K. Simpson* (o/p) on the Greek text has valuable linguistic comments and numerous parallels, but the commentary is stodgy and fails to grapple with the theological thrusts of these epistles. Some find help in *W. Hendriksen* (NTC; see under Thess.). *R. A. Ward* (1974 o/p) is worth scanning, but is not a first choice. He preserves some useful insights for the preacher. Similarly undistinguished but from a less conservative perspective is the commentary by *Arland J. Hultgren* and *Roger Aus* (ACNT; 1984 /$13.95), which strangely lumps together the Pastoral epistles and 2 Thessalonians *Robert J. Karris* does not show off the NTM series at its best (1980 £3.25/$6.95). The EBC divides the Pastorals: 1 and 2 Timothy are treated by *Ralph Earle*, and Titus by *D. Edmond Hiebert* (details in notes on Ephesians). These may be worth a fast skim, but they do not make up in quality what they necessarily lose in brevity.

Popular works abound, of which I mention only two. *H. C. G. Moule* on 2 Timothy has been reprinted (/Kregel 1977 $6.95), but this work sometimes moves from the devotional to the sentimental, and is not one of Moule's better books. John R. W. Stott's *Guard the Gospel* (BST; 1984/1986 £4.50/$11.95) is certainly worth reading.

Indispensable for those who can cope with the language is the fourth edition of the two-volume commentary (898 pp.) by *Ceslaus Spicq* (EtBib; 1969).

Two of the three reprints I mentioned in the third edition of this survey—*Patrick Fairbairn*, orig. 1874; *Charles Erdman*—are again o/p. By contrast, *Henry P. Liddon* on 1 Timothy is still available (/Kregel nd $9.95).

### 3.15 Hebrews

After years of relative neglect, the Epistle to the Hebrews has recently been treated in two magnificent commentaries. *Harold W. Attridge* (Hermeneia; 1989 £30.00/$39.95), on the Greek text, is masterful. Here and there it may tilt a little too far toward Greco-Roman parallels at the expense of Jewish sources, but no serious student of the text can afford to ignore this commentary. My preference, however, is for *William Lane* (WBC, 2 vols.; 1991 /@ $24.99). Not only is this a little more accessible to students and pastors whose Greek is weak than is Attridge's volume, but Lane provides a better mix of technical comment and thoughtful theology. If you can buy only one commentary on Hebrews, buy Lane. Lane's popular-level *Call to Commitment: Responding to the Message of Hebrews* (/Hendrickson repr. 1988 [1985] $7.95) you can circulate around the congregation while you are expounding the text in more detail. The recent NCB volume by *R. McL. Wilson* (1987 /$12.95 pb) is competent and interesting in its own way, but now outstripped by Lane and Attridge.

Until this latest string of commentaries appeared, the two best English works on Hebrews were doubtless those of *F. F. Bruce* (NIC; rev.

ed. 1990 /$27.95) and *Philip E. Hughes* (/Eerdmans 1977 o/p). In some ways the two commentaries complement each other. Bruce provides a great deal of useful information, and writes with caution, but this new revised edition is changed so little from his first edition (1964) that if you already have it there is no point in purchasing the second. In any case, Lane is now to be preferred. The commentary by Hughes focuses less attention on lexical matters and contemporary secondary literature, but it is better than most modern commentaries at surveying the history of interpretation across the entire span of the church, not just the last few decades or centuries. It certainly wrestles with theological questions more thoroughly than does the work by Bruce. That it is now o/p is a serious loss.

The commentary by *H. Montefiore*, published in the same year as the first edition of Bruce (BNTC/HNTC; £8.99 pb / o/p), is stimulating and provocative, but not particularly useful or reliable. At one level, none of these commentaries completely overshadows, for the preacher, *William Barclay* (DSB; rev. ed. 1976 £4.50 pb/$14.95 hb or $8.95 pb). Elsewhere Barclay confesses that Hebrews is one of his favorite parts of Scripture, and he expounds it quite brilliantly, always revealing the practical message of the chapters, but showing more intimacy between Hebrews and Philo than is really warranted. Also worth reading is *Donald A. Hagner* (GNC; Pickering & Inglis 1985 £4.50//NIBC; /Hendrickson 1990 $9.95), although it adds little to the ones already mentioned. Of still less value is the small commentary by *Robert H. Smith* (ACNT; 1984 /$13.95).

For students with the necessary languages, it is essential to explore the Greek text with the French two-volume work by *Ceslaus Spicq* (CNT)—although he makes Philo more important than he really is—and the two German commentaries by *Otto Michel* (MeyerK) and, very recently, *Hans-Friedrich Weiss* (KEK; 1991).

*G. W. Buchanan* (AB; 1972 /$18.00) is a rather strange and offbeat commentary. It sees Messiahship in Hebrews in political terms and the "rest" as entry into the physical land. *F. J. Shierse* (bound with Thessalonians and James; Sheed and Ward/ o/p) sometimes has fresh ways of putting the argument in Hebrews, but is too brief to add much to the larger works. *James Moffatt* (ICC; 1924 £17.50/$29.95), although hardly worth its normal price now that Lane and Attridge have appeared, remains nevertheless a work of considerable learning, and can often be picked up s/h. *B. F. Westcott* (o/p) was doubtless indispensable in its day, but has now been culled by the best recent works. A. Nairne, *The Epistle of Priesthood* (CUP 1921 o/p), consists of a brief commentary with a very long introduction of some 300 pp. Its chief value is perhaps that of explaining the older "sacramental principle" type of theology. *T. Hewitt* (TNTC; o/p) was one of the weakest entries in the old series, and has now been replaced in the new TNTC series by the sturdy work of *Donald Guthrie* (1983 £4.50/$8.95). Thoroughly unrewarding is the work by *Theodore H. Robinson* (Moffatt; o/p). For the commentary by *Simon J. Kistemaker*, see §1.3. *Leon Morris* (EBC vol. 12, running to Revelation; 1981 /$29.95) is worth skimming, but he has not given us his best work. *Paul Ellingworth* (Epworth 1991 £6.95/$12.95) is a useful short commentary, but it usually sheds more light on the use of the language than on the flow of the thought or the theology of the epistle.

F. V. Filson's study *Yesterday* (o/p) aims to shed fresh light on the epistle by viewing it from the vantage point of chapter 13. Among other things it rightly warns against a Platonic interpretation of the "unchanging" Christ. An excellent if somewhat verbose and diffuse rebuttal of the position that sees many Philonic categories in Hebrews is Ronald Williamson's *Philo and the Epistle to the Hebrews* (Brill 1970 o/p). W. Manson's study (not commentary), *The Epistle to the Hebrews* (1951 o/p), is sometimes illuminating, especially in relation to Acts 7, but like all works on Hebrews published before the availability of the Qumran scrolls it is divorced from modern discussion. The use of the OT at Qumran, for instance, has at least some bearing on the use of the OT in Hebrews Nor surprisingly 11QMelch has provoked a long list of studies on the use of Melchizedek in Jewish exegesis, the most important of which is perhaps Fred L. Horton's *The Melchizedek Tradition* (SNTSMS 30; 1976 o/p). Another major study in the same series that repays close reading is the book by David Peterson, *Hebrews and Perfection* (SNTSMS 47; 1982 o/p). Now dated but still stimulating is the provocative work by Ernst Käsemann, *The Wandering People of God* (/Augsburg 1984 o/p). This was written in a period of imprisonment under the Nazis in 1937, when Käsemann was identifying the German radical Confessing Church with the church in Hebrews, understood as the new people of God in its wandering through the wilderness, following the Pioneer and Perfecter of faith. Many of the history-of-religions presuppositions in the work have been eclipsed, and numerous details of exegesis may be questioned. Nevertheless the work is almost as thought-provoking today as when it appeared. Several recent treatments of the "new covenant" theme have appeared, the most important of which is probably that of Susanne Lehne, *The New Covenant in Hebrews* (JSOT 1990 £27.50/$48.00). In one of the last publications before his death, Barnabas Lindars gave us *The Theology of the Letter to the Hebrews* (NTT; 1991 £22.50 hb or £7.95 pb / $29.95 hb). Not only scholars but preachers may well appreciate the critical edition of an old classic by William Perkins, *A Commentary on Hebrews 11* (Pilgrim 1991 [1609 ed.] /$30.00 hb or $19.95 pb).

At the popular and sometimes devotional level, one may still purchase the much reprinted work by Andrew Murray, *The Holiest of All* (/Revell nd $15.95). Quite apart from the doctrinal bias toward "higher life" tradition, the book remains a collection of marvellously pious and spiritually minded gems strung out on a string of abysmal exegesis. More accurate by far is the BST contribution by *Raymond Brown* (1984/1988 £5.95/$11.95). Not to be overlooked is the little work by Robert Jewett, *Letter to Pilgrims* (/Pilgrim 1981 o/p). Jewett did his doctoral study on Hebrews, so he has thought long and hard over this epistle, and there is often some depth in the comments. Occasionally the agenda determines the exegesis, but the work contains some useful reflections on suffering. The old standbys of *H. C. G. Moule* (/Kregel repr. 1977 $5.95) and *Charles Erdman* (/Evangelical Literature League repr. 1987 $4.00) are worth a quick skim. *Louis H. Evans, Jr.* (CC; Word 1986/1985 £7.95/$15.95) is warm but thin; *Rea McDonnell* (MBS; Glazier 1991 £5.95 / Liturgical 1986 $12.95 hb or $7.95 pb) is very thin. There are many other popular treatments, but the busy pastor or student can afford to give most of them a miss.

The Epistle to the Hebrews seems to be a fertile ground for stimulating the reprinting of old commentaries. Of less interest, except to the specialist in the study of Hebrews, are: Robert Anderson's *Types in Hebrews* (/Kregel 1978 $5.95 pb); *A. B. Bruce* (/Kregel nd $17.95 hb); E. W. Bullinger's *Great Cloud of Witnesses in Hebrews Eleven* (/Kregel 1986 [1911] $12.95 pb); *Thomas C. Edwards* (/Kregel nd [1911] $14.95); *Adolph Saphir* (2 vols. in 1; /Kregel 1983 [1875] $22.95). The reprint, 3 vols. in 1, of *William Gouge* (/Kregel nd [1866]) is now itself o/p. The one older work that is still worth a close reading is the two-volume commentary by *Franz Delitzsch*, now regrettably o/p.

### 3.16 James

The three recent large-scale English commentaries on James are by *Peter H. Davids* (NIGTC; 1982 £15.50 hb or £10.50 pb / $19.95 hb); *Sophie Laws* (BNTC/HNTC; 1980 £8.99 / 1981 $19.95); and *Ralph P. Martin* (WBC; 1988 $24.99). Davids is on the Greek text; the latter two can more easily be read by a wider audience. Davids places James in a setting of Jewish messianists in the 50s and 60s; Laws lays out the possibility of a Roman provenance; Martin is a master-piece of condensed writing and an admirable summary of the current status of scholarship on James, but I find myself wanting to qualify his judgments so often that it is not my first choice.

The German commentary by *M. Dibelius* (1928) was revised by *H. Greeven* (1964) and translated to become the entry in the Hermeneia series (1976 £19.00 / 1972 $29.95). Its chief value is the systematic attempt to compare the epistle with other pieces of hortatory litera-ture. Preachers who can cope with Greek may also wish to consult the old standard by *J. B. Mayor* (/Kregel repr.1990 $24.95 hb or $18.95 pb), originally part of the older Macmillan series. The thoroughness of Mayor's work is quite breathtaking, but he is not always as helpful on the practical side as one might desire. The old ICC contribution of *F. J. A. Hort* (1909, as far as 4:7; o/p) and *John H. Ropes* (1924 £17.50/$29.95) is useful for its classical and Hellenistic parallels. The standard German entry is by *F. Mussner* (Herder 3d ed. 1975).

*C. L. Mitton* has written an admirable commentary combining scholarly exegesis and practical insight (1966; unfortunately o/p). The balance is wholly admirable; many other writers are too often content with lame paraphrases of the text. In the same class is the new TNTC contribution by *Douglas J. Moo* (1986 £4.25 / 1987 $6.95). The older and much slimmer TNTC volume was by *R. V. G. Tasker* (1957 o/p). *Peter H. Davids* has given us a slimmer and less techni-cal commentary than the one he prepared for NIGTC, in his contri-bution to NIBC (1989 $9.95 pb). Those who can work with Greek should buy his NIGTC; those who can't, his NIBC. There is no need to buy both. The original NIC contribution was that of *Alexander Ross* (1954 o/p), a book warmly devotional in tone but offering no serious help in the difficult passages). It was replaced by *J. Adamson* (1976 /$22.95), a book somewhat dated even when it appeared, and disproportionately dependent on Hellenistic parallels at the expense of Jewish sources. Adamson has superseded his own work in his recent

*James: The Man and His Message* (/Eerdmans 1989 $24.95 pb). The EBC volume by *Donald W. Burdick* (vol. 12—see on Hebrews; 1981) is unremarkable.

*J. Moffatt* (Moffatt, bound with Peter and Jude; 1928 o/p) sheds some light on the background, but has now been superseded. *E. M. Sidebottom* (NCB, with 2 Peter and Jude; 1982 £5.50 pb / Attic 1967 $7.50 or Eerdmans 1982 $8.95) is disappointing and very thin where comment is most needed. *Bo Reike* (AB, with Peter and Jude; 2d ed. 1964 /$18.00 pb) is somewhat better, but now eclipsed by Davids, Laws, and Moo.

I have not usually mentioned the *Helps for Translators* series put out by UBS, since most of the volumes, although doubtless helpful to translators, are so thin on background and theology that they are of minimal use to students and preachers. But *Robert G. Bratcher* on James, Peter, and Jude (1983 /$10.00) offers good value for money. The CC commentary by *Paul A. Cedar* on James, 1–2 Peter, and Jude (1984 np) offers application, but little exegesis, and even in the former, Mitton is often more incisive.

Popular commentaries on James abound. *Curtis Vaughan* (/Zondervan nd $6.95 pb) is worth scanning; *Richard Kugelman* (NTM; 1981 £2.45/$5.95) just barely. *R. A. Martin* and *John H. Elliott* (ACNT on James, Peter, and Jude; 1982 /$13.95) offers competent digests of exegeses, but is too brief to be very helpful and sometimes too speculative to be very convincing. The exposition by *J. Alec Motyer* (BST; 1985 £5.75 / 1988 $11.95) displays the strengths we have come to expect from this series.

Useful reprints include, in addition to those already mentioned, the commentary by *Robert Johnstone* (BoT repr. 1977 /$19.95), the expository lectures from the last century by *Rudolf E. Stier* (/Kregel nd 1982 [1871] $12.95), and *Thomas Manton*'s classic (BoT 1968 £6.95 / repr. 1983 $19.95).

## 3.17  1 Peter

Except in a couple of instances, I shall not mention commentaries incorporated with James.

The fullest commentary in English at the exegetical level is that of *J. Ramsey Michaels* (WBC; 1988 /$24.99). Michaels tentatively dates this epistle to the last quarter of the first century; occasionally this affects his exegesis, but not often. Michaels has also contributed the Word

Biblical Themes volume (1989 np). *Peter Davids* (NIC; 1990 /$24.95)
is competent and clear. On *Simon J. Kistemaker*, see notes at §1.3.

The standard work on the Greek text is that of *E. G. Selwyn*
(Macmillan 1946; o/p). This is one of the monumental pieces of
industry that characterized the earlier Macmillan series. Most later
commentaries have depended heavily on Selwyn. Hard on its heels
came the work by *F. W. Beare* (1947 o/p), who rejects Petrine authorship and argues for a late date. Nevertheless the book is full of exegetical insight. In the third edition (1970 o/p), Beare's commentary
shows more dependence on continental emphases on the putative
liturgical origins of the epistle. Older works on the Greek text, including *C. A. Bigg* (ICC; 1902 £17.50/$29.95), have been superseded.
*J. Moffatt* (see under James) is concise and penetrating, primarily with
respect to the actual situation of the original readers, but his work is
now badly dated.

*J. N. D. Kelly* (BNTC/HNTC, on Peter and Jude; 1969 $9.95
pb / Baker repr. 1981 $14.95 pb) is very useful. It is thoughtful and
sensitive in elucidating the thought of the epistles, and brings out
connections between 1 and 2 Peter. *Ernest Best* (NCB; 1982 £5.95/
$10.95) is also a good commentary, but not better than Kelly or
Davids, let alone Michaels. *C. E. B. Cranfield* (TBC with 2 Peter and
Jude; 1960 o/p) is fresh and almost always useful, but too brief to
displace the larger works. *A. M. Hunter*'s commentary in IB volume 12 (1957 £21.50 or £240.00 the set / $324.50 the set) is also
useful. *A. M. Stibbs* (TNTC; 1959 o/p) is full of practical insights,
but has now been replaced by *Wayne Grudem* (1988 £4.50/$6.95).
This is an independent exegesis (it interacts with little of the secondary
literature) always worth consulting. Scholars and preachers alike will
find the lengthy appendix on the "spirits in prison" passage to war-
rant the price of the book. *Donald Senior* on the Petrine epistles (NTM;
1980 £3.25/$10.95 hb or $6.95 pb) is clearly written but brief and
unremarkable. Something similar must be said for *Edwin A. Blum*
(EBC vol.12; see Morris on Hebrews).

The rise of sociological approaches to the NT is nowhere more
clearly in evidence than in the modern study of 1 Peter. The commentary that generated not a little of this discussion is the German
work by *Leonhard Goppelt* (MeyerK; 1978), which Eerdmans is apparently going to bring out in English in due course. Goppelt's work is
competent and detailed, and, apart from spurring sociological
approaches, it is rich in making links both to the Dead Sea Scrolls

and to the OT. In English the study that has precipitated sociological approaches to 1 Peter is that of John H. Elliott, *A Home for the Homeless* (1981 o/p). Although at many points it is suggestive, the thesis is overdone, and there are too few controls applied to the selection of sociological models. But treated with reserve the approach has some value.

The older four-volume devotional work by *Robert Leighton* (o/p) is worth skimming if you can read fast, but it is extraordinarily long for so short an epistle. The expository discourses of *John Brown* have been reprinted at various times. At the moment, the only one in print, so far as I know, is his *2 Peter Chapter 1: Parting Counsels* (BoT 1980 £7.95/). *Gordon H. Clark* on the Petrine epistles (1980 o/p) can be thoughtful, sometimes frustrating, and almost never humble, but occasionally a useful supplement to the standard works.

Popular commentaries abound. The best by far is the BST entry by *Edmund P. Clowney* (1988 £5.95 / 1989 $11.95). Perhaps I should mention two others: *Jay E. Adams* (1979 o/p), and *Paul A. Cedar* (CC; see on James). *John Lillie*'s lectures on the Petrine epistles were reprinted by Klock and Klock in 1978, but they are again o/p. The commentary by *Martin Luther* on the epistles of Peter and Jude has been reprinted (/Kregel 1982 $10.95 pb).

### 3.18 2 Peter and Jude

Except in one or two instances, I shall not mention commentaries already discussed under James or 1 Peter, of which there are many (see especially Kelly, Cranfield, Moffatt, Reicke, Sidebottom, and Bigg).

By far the best work on 2 Peter and Jude is the exhaustive commentary by *Richard J. Bauckham* (WBC; 1983 /$22.99). There is no relevant literature up to his time that Bauckham has not considered, and he here puts to good use his knowledge of the so-called Jewish intertestamental literature, as well as some of the more recent Gnostic finds. Why he concluded that 2 Peter is pseudonymous is still not clear to me: his evidence does not strike me as very convincing. But this point should not put anyone off using what will be the standard in the field for decades to come.

A brief but admirable treatment of these two short epistles is found in *E. M. B. Green* (TNTC; revised ed. in 1987). On the Greek text, although *J. B. Mayor*'s massive commentary has often been reprinted (most recently by /Baker 1979), it is again o/p. The work of *D. Edmond Hiebert* (/Bob Jones University Press 1989 $12.95) works reverently through the text, but adds little of substance to Bauckham. The work of *Thomas Manton* on Jude has been reprinted both by BoT (1989 [1658 ed.] £6.95/$15.95) and by Kregel (nd /$20.95 hb or $14.95 pb).

## 3.19 Johannine Epistles

The two major commentaries in English are both very full indeed—almost too full for some preachers who perhaps devote too little time to sermon preparation. In both instances the pastor will have to learn what sections to skim and what sections to read with minute care. The first is by *Raymond E. Brown* (AB; 1983 £30.00 / 1982 $28.00 pb)—a mammoth book that complements the author's two-volume commentary on John. Brown has moved his position somewhat since writing his volumes on the Fourth Gospel. He is far more sure he can delineate the history of the Johannine community (cf. his *The Community of the Beloved Disciple*) than he used to be, and he is less certain that the writer of the Johannine epistles (whom he does not take to be the author of the Fourth Gospel) is a faithful interpreter of the Fourth Gospel. To put the matter another way, he is far more generous with the opponents John confronts in the Epistles than seems warranted by the actual evidence. What is distinctive (and frankly unbelievable) in his exegesis of these epistles is that everything in 1 John is understood to have specific reference to the Fourth Gospel and its (mis)interpretation by the opponents. Nevertheless the exegetical comments are incisive, the bibliography invaluable. The other major work is by *Stephen S. Smalley* (WBC; 1984 /$22.99). The bibliography is as good, and Smalley is at his best when he is summarizing and interacting with the positions of others. This work is a little more conservative than that of Brown (though I do not find Smalley's reconstruction of the setting very believable), but the comments themselves are not as incisive.

Four other recent commentaries, written on a smaller scale, deserve notice. *Kenneth Grayston* (NCB; 1984 £9.95/$10.95) is too brief to be a first choice, but is of some value because of its provocative positions (e.g., Grayston thinks the Johannine epistles were written before the Fourth Gospel). Of much more value to the preacher is *I. Howard Marshall* (NIC; 1978 /$19.95). The book is simply written, and ably brings together a good deal of previous scholarship without getting bogged down in minutiae. In my view Marshall's theological commitments, in line with his book *Kept by the Power of God*, determine the exegesis here and there, but this is a very good commentary. The ACNT contribution by *Robert Kysar* (1986 /$13.95) is workmanlike and competent, but not nearly as full. On *Simon J. Kistemaker*, see comments at §1.3.

One of the most useful conservative commentaries on these epistles, so far as the preacher is concerned, is still that of *J. R. W. Stott* (TNTC; rev. ed. 1988 £4.50/). It is packed with both exegetical comments and thoughtful application, and was the best in the old TNTC series. It is good to see it revised and holding its own in the new TNTC. *C. H. Dodd* (Moffatt; 1946 o/p) is highly praised by almost everyone, but I find it difficult to see why. The quality of his prose is superb, but he is so bound to his old-fashioned liberal tradition that on point after point he is wildly out of sympathy with the text. He insists, for instance, that John's quick definition "sin is lawlessness" is shallow, that 2 John must be condemned for its "fierce intolerance," and so forth.

Two older commentaries retain some importance. *B. F. Westcott* on the Greek text has been periodically reprinted, but is now o/p; *A. E. Brooke* (ICC; 1912 £7.50/$29.95) is still available. The latter was a standard in its day, but the best of its notes and comments have been picked up by the more recent works. *J. L. Houlden* (BNTC/HNTC; 1973 £10.99 pb / 1974 $10.95 [also repr. /Hendrickson 1987 $19.95!]) is so caustic that he is more irritating than edifying. The Hermeneia series has been guilty of very bad judgment in some of its entries, and the choice in this case was one of them: *Rudolf Bultmann*'s ET (1973 £15.00/$22.95) is so brief, and so concerned with improbable source criticism, that its remaining exegetical comments are not worth the price. *Gordon H. Clark* (1980 o/p) is better on these epistles than on some others, but he shapes quite a bit of his argument against Bultmann, and on these epistles I doubt if Bultmann is influential enough to be worth the trouble.

Two important studies, sane, cautious, insightful, are by Judith Lieu: *The Second and Third Epistles of John: History and Background* (T & T Clark 1986 £16.95/$34.95), and *The Theology of the Johannine Epistles* (NTT; 1991 £22.50 hb or £7.95 pb/$29.95 hb or $10.95 pb). The most recent major German commentary is by *Georg Strecker* (KEK; 1989 DM 98), but in some ways the older work by

*Rudolf Schnackenburg* (HTKNT; 5th ed. 1975) is a superior commentary. One regrets that it has never been translated.

The recent commentary by *Donald W. Burdick* (/Moody 1985 o/p) is not to be overlooked, although not always to be trusted. Almost 500 pp. in length, the book attempts to offer exegesis of the Greek text theological comment, present-day application, and some comments on structure. Although rarely innovative or fresh, the book will help some students think their way from text to theology to sermon. But beware the mechanical and clearly mistaken understanding of Greek tenses and their significance. This work is not to be confused with his purely popular commentary on these epistles (/Moody 1970 $5.95 pb). Two older classics are Robert Law's *The Tests of Life* (regrettably o/p), and George B. Findlay's *Studies in John's Epistles: Fellowship in the Life Eternal* (/Kregel repr. 1989 [1909] $19.95 hb or $13.95 pb). Both of these works are eminently quotable, but they have been culled by more recent writers, notably Stott. The little commentary by *F. F. Bruce* (Pickering & Inglis 1978 £2.95 / Eerdmans rev. ed. 1990 $8.95 pb) is a series of studies first published as articles in *The Witness*, and is well worth reading. The essays that make up most of R. E. O. White's *An Open Letter to Evangelicals: A Devotional and Homiletical Commentary on the First Epistle of John* (o/p) are well written but theologically tepid when compared with 1 John itself, but the "Notes" on the text at the end of the book are excellent.

Popular works abound. Among the better ones are *J. W. Roberts* (/Abilene Christian University Press 1984 $12.95) and *R. Alan Culpepper* (KPG; 1985 /$6.95 pb). In 1982, Klock and Klock reprinted the massive work (612 pp.) of *J. Morgan* and *S. Cox*, but it is again o/p. So also is *Alfred Plummer*—in any case not his finest hour.

## 3.20 Revelation

Of the writing of books on Revelation there is no end. Mercifully, several excellent commentaries are available to compensate for a great deal of nonsense one finds elsewhere. One of the preacher's or student's first requirements, before plunging into the "application," is to find a couple of commentators who understand the nature and purpose of apocalyptic. In this respect, we might might wisely turn to *G. B. Caird* (BNTC/HNTC; 1985 £10.99 / 1966 $19.95) or *G. R. Beasley-Murray* (NCB; 1981 £9.95/$12.95). But Revelation also represents the prophetic tradition, and this is underlined by *Leon Morris* (TNTC; rev. ed. 1987 £4.50/$8.95) and *George Ladd* (/Eerdmans 1971 $12.95 pb). Perhaps the best single volume is that of *Robert H. Mounce* (NIC; 1977 /$22.95)—a learned but well-written work that not only explains the text satisfactorily in most instances but also introduces the student to the best of the secondary literature. Not to be overlooked is the work of *J. P. Sweet*, listed with the Pelican series on the British side (1979 £20.00 hb or £9.50 pb) and now with TPINT on the American (1990 $24.95). Longer than most contributions to the Pelican series, this commentary is insightful at many points, and includes an able discussion of the degree of persecution that did (or did not!) take place under Emperor Domitian.

*Josephine Massyngberde Ford* (AB; 1975 /$22.00 pb) is entertaining, primarily because it is eccentric. John the Baptist, we are told, was responsible for most of Revelation—but perhaps that is not too surprising from a scholar who has argued that the Blessed Virgin penned Hebrews. Her background material, especially from Qumran, would have been invaluable, had more of her references been right: in one section I checked, fully one-third of the references were incorrect. After being o/p for some years, Austin Farrar's *The Rebirth of Images* is enjoying another good run (/Peter Smith nd [1949] $13.25). It too is idiosyncratic, its title betraying the key it offers to help readers interpret Revelation; but it is strangely powerful and evocative. Paul S. Minear's *I Saw a New Earth* (1968 o/p) draws on sound biblical scholarship to show the relevance of Revelation to the present day—although "present day" is becoming dated. More difficult to assess in brief compass is David Chilton's *The Days of Vengeance: An Exposition of the Book of Revelation* (/Dominion 1987). The book is strongest where it brings together from larger, more technical commentaries something of the wealth of OT allusions, and shows their relevance to the interpretation of the Apocalypse. But Chilton ties his interpretation of the entire book to a dogmatic insistence that it was written before A.D. 70, and that its predictions are focused on the destruction of Jerusalem. Although there are some excellent theological links crafted in this book, the central setting and argument are so weak and open to criticism that I cannot recommend the work very warmly. The lengthy (18 pp.) "Publisher's Preface" by Gary North is so arrogant and condescending it is embarrassing: I earnestly hope Chilton found it so.

The traditional conservative commentary in many circles until fairly recently was W. Hendriksen's *More Than Conquerors* (1982 [1939] $14.95). In some circles this book has been assigned almost legendary value, but one must assume that the reason lies primarily in the combination of sober interpretation and evangelical fervor, all of it easily accessible, at a time when evangelicals were not producing much of worth on Revelation. It is now entirely eclipsed by more recent commentaries. *W. Barclay* (DSB, 2 vols.; 1976 @ £4.50 / @ $12.95 hb or $7.95 pb) is still of some practical value. *Alan F. Johnson* (EBC vol. 12; see Morris on Hebrews) has written the best commentary in this volume of EBC. *Ludwig van Hartingsveld* (/Eerdmans 1986 $8.95 pb), translated from the Dutch, offers virtually no interaction with other views (a "must" for a useful commentary on a book like Revelation), and provides little grist for the modern expositor (despite the subtitle of this new series: "Text and Interpretation: A Practical Commentary"). *Sean P. Kealy* (Glazier 1991 £9.95 / Liturgical 1987 $12.95) offers in fairly short space a lot of clear, interpretative help at the historical level, but the author finally endorses so existentialist an interpretation that much of the good is vitiated. *Philip Edgcumbe Hughes* (IVP/Eerdmans 1990 £13.95/$17.95) is too short to be anyone's first choice. It bodes well to replace Hendriksen. Although Hughes has many of the themes right, in my view he has the interpretation of not a few passages wrong. There is little interaction with other literature.

*H. B. Swete* on the Greek text has often been reprinted, but is now again o/p. Normally Swete is stodgy and often dull, but although he never shakes off his pedestrianism, in this commentary there is some really useful and thorough material that helps the reader to see the depth of the book. *M. Kiddle* (Moffatt; o/p) is simply too verbose: the sum of its fruitful comment hardly justifies the number of pages it occupies.

Three experts on Revelation toward the beginning of the century were *R. H. Charles* (ICC, 2 vols.; 1920 @ £19.95 / $29.95 and $34.95 respectively), *Isbon T. Beckwith* (Macmillan 1922 o/p), and, to a lesser extent, *W. Milligan* (EB; 1891 o/p). Charles in particular should not be overlooked, in view of the immense scholarship it represents. In one sense it has not been surpassed, but the preacher should not set too much hope on it, as the two volumes are very technical and only rarely practical. Beckwith is almost as good, and more accessible to those who have a command of Greek. Milligan oscillates between the excellent and the disappointing. *James Moffatt* (EGNT, 5 vols.; /Eerdmans 1952 $89.95 the set) still repays study. *Martin Rist* (IB; see §1.23 for details) claims to offer one or two completely original thoughts, but there is no dearth of scholars who claim to do this on the Book of Revelation.

Not a commentary but a stimulating collection of essays is found in Elisabeth Schüssler Fiorenza's *The Book of Revelation: Justice and Judgment* (Fortress 1984 £11.50 pb/$12.95 pb), who follows Käsemann in understanding apocalyptic in terms of power. Colin J. Hemer's *The Letters to the Seven Churches of Asia* (JSOT 1986 £22.50 hb or £10.50 pb / $32.50 hb) is by far the most detailed and evenhanded study of Rev. 2–3, steeped in suggestive details, although of course the preacher will have to draw the appropriate applications. Leonard L. Thompson's *The Book of Revelation: Apocalypse and Empire* (OUP 1990 £24.00/$29.95) is a series of useful essays tracing many of Revelation's themes against the background of the social history and politics of the period.

There is no end of shorter or lighter commentaries. The standard dispensational commentary today is probably still that of *John F. Walvoord* (/Moody 1966 $17.95). *Elisabeth Schüssler Fiorenza* (ProcC; 1991 /$13.95) and *James L. Blevins* (KPG; 1984 £4.95/$6.95) are both so brief that they deserve no more than a quick skim. *Charles H. Giblin* (/Liturgical 1991 $9.95) is designed for laypeople, and is organized around the theme of "God's holy war of liberation." *M. Eugene Boring* in the Interpretation series (/Westminster & John Knox 1989 $18.95) has much more substance, although Boring sometimes tries to import his views on the prophetic words of the exalted Jesus into the text. William Still's *A Vision of Glory: An Exposition of the Book of Revelation* (Nicholas Gray 1987 £3.95/) is a slim volume that will help some laypeople. In fact there are scores of slim or popular expositions, some of them reliable but too thin to be useful to the preacher, many of them fanciful. One of the really excellent popular treatments, however much one might want to disagree with this or that detail, is the BST volume by Michael Wilcock, *I Saw Heaven Opened: The Message of Revelation* (1984 £5.75 / 1988 $9.95). One should not overlook the popularization Robert H. Mounce has provided of his NIC commentary in *What Are We Waiting For? A Commentary on Revelation* (/Eerdmans 1992 $10.95). This may give the preacher some practical hints, but it should not be used without careful reading of the NIC volume.

# 4

# Some "Best Buys"

This brief list does not pretend to identify which is the "best" commentary on every NT book: the opening pages of this survey have already made it clear that what is "best" can vary from reader to reader, and depends in any case on what kind of information a particular reader is looking for—quite apart from the theological orientation of particular commentaries. The following rather subjective list identifies commentaries that are good value for money for the theological student or well-trained preacher who is interested in understanding the Scriptures, and who is willing to read commentaries critically.

| | |
|---|---|
| Matthew | W. D. Davies & D. C. Allison for advanced students; R. T. France or R. H. Mounce |
| Mark | W. Lane; also C. E. B. Cranfield |
| Luke | J. A. Fitzmyer or I. H. Marshall for advanced students; W. L. Liefeld or L. Morris |
| John | C. K. Barrett; L. Morris |
| Acts | R. N. Longenecker; I. H. Marshall |
| Romans | C. E. B. Cranfield for advanced students; wait for D. J. Moo; also F. F. Bruce; C. K. Barrett; A. Nygren |

| | |
|---|---|
| 1 Corinthians | G. D. Fee; C. K. Barrett |
| 2 Corinthians | C. K. Barrett |
| Galatians | F. F. Bruce; R. N. Longenecker |
| Ephesians | A. T. Lincoln; C. L. Mitton; A. G. Patzia |
| Philippians | P. T. O'Brien; M. Silva |
| Colossians/Philemon | P. T. O'Brien |
| Thessalonians | C. A. Wanamaker; F. F. Bruce |
| Pastorals | J. N. D. Kelly; G. D. Fee; J. D. Quinn on Titus; wait for G. Knight |
| Hebrews | W. Lane |
| James | P. H. Davids in NIGTC or NIBC; D. J. Moo |
| 1 Peter | J. R. Michaels or P. H. Davids; J. N. D. Kelly; W. Grudem |
| 2 Peter and Jude | R. Bauckham |
| Johannine Epistles | R. E. Brown or S. S. Smalley for advanced students; I. H. Marshall; J. R. W. Stott |
| Revelation | R. H. Mounce |